Praise for *The Triangle of Truth*

"A paradigm shift that has the power to change everything! *The Triangle of Truth* is ancient wisdom on a twenty-first-century platform."
　　—Marshall Goldsmith, author of *What Got You Here Won't Get You There*

"Lisa McLeod does for relationships what Steven Covey did for work habits. *The Triangle of Truth* teaches you how to better connect with customers and *close* more business. If you're serious about success, you need to read this book."
　　—Suzanne Harchelroad, director of sales for Kimberly-Clark Corporation

"Every CEO in America should read this book! Lisa Earle McLeod unlocks the secret of ending turf wars and creating a culture of accountability, candor, and creativity. Whether you work with one person or thousands, *The Triangle of Truth* is a must-read for anyone who wants their team to become more successful."
　　—Keith Ferrazzi, author of *Who's Got Your Back* and *Never Eat Alone*

"*The Triangle of Truth* reveals how you can rise above to create stronger relationships, families, and careers. In a remarkably quick read, Lisa Earle McLeod shows you how to elevate."
　　—Tom Rath, author of *How Full Is Your Bucket?*

"We trained our entire sales and leadership team in this model. *The Triangle of Truth* enables us to approach our customers from a different angle. Our team is better prepared, and our customers *love* it!"
　　—Lisa Siddle, learning and development, Cap G Limited

"*The Triangle of Truth* illustrates how your inner-thought track determines your success, or lack of success. Lisa shows you which inner dialogues attract customers and colleagues and which ones turn people off. As a leader and coach in a highly competitive field, I strongly recommend you read this book and buy it for your people."
　　—Robin Dogas, Medical Action Industries

continued ...

D0288663

"Most 'truths' about life are simple when you figure them out, and life is often very complicated until you do. In *The Triangle of Truth*, Lisa Earle McLeod describes and profusely illustrates the futility and destructiveness of either/or thinking and with equally profuse illustrations offers a startlingly simple third option—*And.* "

—Harville Hendrix, PhD, author of *Getting the Love You Want*

"Lisa Earle McLeod is one funny, brainy, perceptive woman. *The Triangle of Truth* distills her natural wisdom into a bubbly pick-me-up that will make you feel better all day. Buy the book, and grab a chance to ride on Lisa's uplifting energy." —Martha Beck, *O, the Oprah Magazine*

"Most of the mischief in our lives and in the world comes from our egregious inability to be both absolutely honest and absolutely respectful with each other at the same time. Lisa McLeod offers powerful, practical, and timely solutions to help us dramatically improve our lives and our organizations by striking at the root of this pernicious problem."

—Joseph Grenny, author of *Influencer* and *Crucial Conversations*

"In this ingeniously written book, Lisa shows us how to forever do away with the 'false dilemma,' the unnecessary use of the word 'or,' and instead find the best alternative. No, not compromise, not forgo your values or desires, but to step it up a notch and create a bigger pie for everyone." —Bob Burg, coauthor of *The Go-Giver* and *Endless Referrals*

"*The Triangle of Truth* is what comes out of the book oven when an extraordinary word chef like Lisa McLeod blends humor Cosby would envy with wisdom Buddha espoused and then adds a heaping cup of hit-you-where-you-live realism. You may giggle and sniffle but you will never be the same after reading this great book."

—Chip R. Bell, author of *Take Their Breath Away*

"I love this book! Lisa gives us a perspective on relationships and communication that can (and will) change peoples' lives."

—Joe Calloway, business consultant and author of *A Class Of One*

THE
TRIANGLE
OF TRUTH

The Surprisingly Simple Secret to
Resolving Conflicts Large and Small

Lisa Earle McLeod

A Perigee Book

A PERIGEE BOOK
Published by the Penguin Group
Penguin Group (USA) Inc.
375 Hudson Street, New York, New York 10014, USA

Penguin Group (Canada), 90 Eglinton Avenue East, Suite 700, Toronto, Ontario M4P 2Y3, Canada (a division of Pearson Penguin Canada Inc.)
Penguin Books Ltd., 80 Strand, London WC2R 0RL, England
Penguin Group Ireland, 25 St. Stephen's Green, Dublin 2, Ireland (a division of Penguin Books Ltd.)
Penguin Group (Australia), 250 Camberwell Road, Camberwell, Victoria 3124, Australia (a division of Pearson Australia Group Pty. Ltd.)
Penguin Books India Pvt. Ltd., 11 Community Centre, Panchsheel Park, New Delhi—110 017, India
Penguin Group (NZ), 67 Apollo Drive, Rosedale, North Shore 0632, New Zealand (a division of Pearson New Zealand Ltd.)
Penguin Books (South Africa) (Pty.) Ltd., 24 Sturdee Avenue, Rosebank, Johannesburg 2196, South Africa
Penguin Books Ltd., Registered Offices: 80 Strand, London WC2R 0RL, England

While the author has made every effort to provide accurate telephone numbers and Internet addresses at the time of publication, neither the publisher nor the author assumes any responsibility for errors, or for changes that occur after publication. Further, the publisher does not have any control over and does not assume any responsibility for author or third-party websites or their content.

PRINTING HISTORY
Perigee hardcover edition / January 2010
Perigee trade paperback edition / February 2011

Perigee trade paperback ISBN: 978-0-399-53643-4

The Library of Congress has cataloged the Perigee hardcover edition as follows:

McLeod, Lisa Earle.
    The triangle of truth : the surprisingly simple secret to resolving conflicts large and small / Lisa Earle McLeod.— 1st ed.
        p.   cm.
    ISBN 978-0-399-53567-3
    1. Interpersonal conflict.   2. Conflict management.   3. Problem solving.   4. Conflict (Psychology)   I. Title.
    BF637.I48M43 2010
    303.6'9—dc22   2009032250

PRINTED IN THE UNITED STATES OF AMERICA

10 9 8 7 6 5 4 3 2 1

Most Perigee books are available at special quantity discounts for bulk purchases for sales promotions, premiums, fund-raising, or educational use. Special books, or book excerpts, can also be created to fit specific needs. For details, write: Special Markets, Penguin Group (USA) Inc., 375 Hudson Street, New York, New York 10014.

For You,
Because you are nothing short of magnificent

CONTENTS

PRINCIPLE 3: HOLD SPACE FOR OTHER PERSPECTIVES   61
Solving the Your Agenda Versus
My Agenda Quagmire

PRINCIPLE 4: SEEK HIGHER GROUND   105
How to Rise Above the Comfort and
Convenience of False Choices

PRINCIPLE 5: DISCERN INTENT   143
Discovering the Real Truth Behind Imperfect Solutions

PRINCIPLE 6: ELEVATE OTHERS   171
*How to Change the Way Other People Think and
Why You Should Even Bother to Try*

What Do Mary Kay, Buddha, and Elvis Know That You Don't?

Buddha called it the Middle Path and told the monks it was the key to enlightenment.

Albert Einstein used it to reconcile competing beliefs about science and religion.

Admiral James Stockdale employed it to survive seven and a half years of torture at the Hanoi Hilton.

Mary Kay Ash made it a foundation of her business and created a cosmetics empire.

Barack Obama applied the concept to politics and catapulted into the Oval Office.

Elvis Presley became the King of Rock 'n' Roll when he used it to combine "black" music with "white" music and create a sound like nobody had ever heard before.

It's a concept that is both old and new. It's a dramatically different way of thinking that can transform your work, your family, your relationships, your life, and, quite frankly, our planet.

I call it the **Triangle of Truth**. It's the ability to hold two seemingly conflicting ideas in your mind at the same time, and assimilate them in a way that makes their whole greater than the sum of their parts.

I didn't invent it so much as I stumbled upon it. But it's one of those discoveries that once someone points it out for you, you begin to see evidence of it everywhere you turn.

It's both conceptual and practical, and while it draws on the wisdom of the past, it also points us in a new direction for the future.

The Triangle of Truth is how one side can be right, without making the other side wrong.

It's why our forefathers organized a government around the competing concepts of freedom and responsibility.

It's why Eastern and Western medicine are finally assimilating into holistic health.

It's why individuals and organizations that embrace both masculine and feminine energy have a spiritual and economic advantage over those who don't.

And it's why people who can see the big picture experience more love, peace, and happiness than those who spend all their energy defending a narrow point of view.

The Triangle of Truth is an elegantly simple model that applies to everything from business and relationships to politics and religion. It elevates your thinking to a higher level.

Here's how it works: No doubt you've heard the expression, there are two sides to every argument. It doesn't matter whether it's the abortion debate or an argument over who gets the last piece of pumpkin pie at Thanksgiving dinner; there are usually two differing points of view.

It's like a line, with one side on the right and the other on the left. Both parties are convinced their perspective is the only correct one, so they direct most of their energy toward trying to convince that other person to move over to their side of the line, or at the very least trying to convince the rest of the world that theirs is the real truth.

My Truth   **Your Truth**

Traditional problem-solving models suggest that compromise is the answer. Both parties learn to give a little and they try to come together on a middle ground.

If you're talking about something as simple as pumpkin pie, it usually works.

Middle Ground Compromise

Half a piece of pie

I want a whole piece of pie   You want a whole piece of pie

One of you cuts it in half and the other chooses the first piece. Sure, it's not as nice as having a big ole wedge of pie all to yourself. But a little sugar beats no sugar, and who wants to fight about pie on Thanksgiving when you could be taking a nap?

But when it comes to more contentious issues like abortion, religion, or whether or not the toilet seat should stay up or down, sometimes there is no middle ground.

That's where the triangle comes in. Instead of trying to compromise in the middle, or the more common scenario, fight about who's right and who's wrong, the Triangle of Truth provides a model for redirecting your energy. It points you toward a solution at the top of the triangle that honors the truth on both sides.

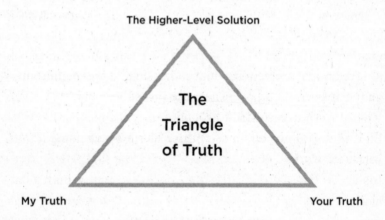

It's easy to understand, but it can be challenging to implement. Problems like abortion and religious conflicts don't have readily apparent solutions, and sometimes we're so mired in our own perspective that we are blinded to any truths the other side may be offering.

Yet for those who master it—or even get it partly right— the Triangle of Truth can be a game-changing mind-shift that transforms the way you think about everything, and everyone.

It can help you create more happiness and success, and it can improve your relationship with every single person you know. That's because the Triangle of Truth is a tool that enables you to solve conflicts, big and small, without the drama and angst. It's a way of thinking that enables you to rise above the either/ or debates that stymie so many of our endeavors, and to instead create the kind of environment you want and deserve.

The Triangle of Truth allows you to step outside of yourself. It enables you to become more than just your thoughts and ideas. And it can help you move toward your highest potential.

Sounds like big stuff, I know. Trust me, I didn't start out with such lofty aspirations. In fact, when I first came up with the Triangle of Truth model, I wasn't thinking about human potential at all. I was thinking about sex, politics, and why my husband and neighbors were driving me nuts.

It all started during the 2004 election. For the record, it was Bush versus Kerry, but it could have just as easily been Nixon versus McGovern or the Yankees versus the Red Sox or Brutus versus Caesar. The battle lines had been drawn. Both sides claimed to be the party of God and country, and anyone who opposed them was just wrong, wrong, wrong. I had an opinion, as I usually do, but I was in the minority on this round. Most of my neighbors were voting for the other guy, and after a few go-nowhere arguments, I decided that life in suburbia would be easier if I learned to muzzle my mouth. But inwardly, oh how I seethed. I couldn't believe that the people I once thought of as intelligent human beings had gone so insane. Clearly I was a terrible judge of character, because if these people had any sense whatsoever they would never be voting for that guy.

However, as frustrated as I was with the people I once

considered my peers, I was even more annoyed with my husband. Not because of politics—for once we actually agreed on that—but because of our differing views of what constitutes intimacy in a marriage.

On one side of the fence, or perhaps more accurately, one side of the bed, was my husband, a man who had patiently settled for dribs and drabs of romance during the baby years, but who was becoming increasingly frustrated because—despite getting two kids out of diapers—he was not, shall we say, feasting on a sexual bounty from his wife.

Now I like sex, I swear, I really do. In fact, there was a time in our lives when I used to actually initiate it. But at that stage, I was so exhausted from my job and the kids that I couldn't even see straight. I'm embarrassed to admit this, but I had begun to think of my husband as a bit of a sexual pest. I found myself wondering why the man who never wanted to share his inner thoughts during dinner was so eager to cuddle up to me at night.

As with many couples, we were stressed to the max, and the peripherals, anything not at the absolute top of our list, fell by the wayside. For me it was sex, for him it was talking. I wanted more of one, and he wanted more of the other. It's a common marital quagmire, and while it doesn't always fall along our oh-so-very typical male and female battle lines, the hundreds of emotional emails I get whenever I write about this subject tell me that we're hardly the first couple to experience this problem.

That didn't stop us both from taking it personally. Surely if our partner really loved us he or she would want more of X, rather than just Y. Because Y without X was no kind of marriage at all, and the fact that we had to actually ask (or in some cases beg) for this one very important thing was proof that he/she probably never really cared in the first place.

I'd laugh at the self-imposed drama if I hadn't spent the better part of a decade embroiled in it.

As we alternatively bickered, sulked, whined, and felt unloved, it gradually dawned on me that we were doing the exact same thing as the politicians. As often happens when people feel like they're being wronged, we each became so convinced of our own righteousness that we were literally blind to the truth of what our partner was saying. Just like the warring politicians, we were act-

> **We were acting as though we had competing agendas when in fact we had complementary ones.**

ing as though we had competing agendas when in fact we had complementary ones.

And thus the Triangle of Truth was born. In the midst of a stagnating marriage and a polarized election, I finally realized that there was another way.

Albert Einstein said, "We cannot solve the problems of today with the level of thinking that created them." The Triangle of Truth is the more-talking, more-sex solution. It's a way to move beyond the argument and elevate your thinking. It's a way to honor the other person without compromising yourself. It allows you to cut through the clutter and the emotional drama and discern the real truth in any situation.

In the case of my marriage, the real truth was, my husband

didn't want just a little more sex and romance, he wanted a lot more; and I didn't want just a little talking, I wanted a lot. Compromise didn't work because it always wound up feeling like some sort of tit-for-tat (pun intended) exchange. Who wants to be married to someone who only talks or sleeps with you so that you'll do more of the other thing with them?

In reality, I didn't want my husband to feel forced to talk with me; I wanted him to *want* to talk with me. And while a man may settle for duty sex—and believe me, my husband did on more than one occasion—what he really wanted was a wife who wanted him just as badly as he wanted her.

The Triangle of Truth gave us a way to both be right.

Did we morph into a talk-all-night, share-all-your-inner-thoughts, give-public-workshops-on-Tantric-sex couple? Well, not all at once. But you'd be amazed at how quickly things change when you validate another person's truth. When I was finally able to put aside my anger, look my husband in the eye, and tell him that I thought sex was one of the best parts of marriage and that we should make it a bigger priority, he practically teared up. When he told me that I was his favorite person to talk with, I could literally feel my heart begin to soften.

That's why the Triangle of Truth works, because it redirects your energy, away from the fighting, toward a more all-encompassing solution. It allows you to create a whole that is greater than the sum of its parts.

> The Triangle of Truth works because it redirects your energy, away from the fighting, toward a more all-encompassing solution. It allows you to create a whole that is greater that the sum of its parts.

It's why Buddha told the monks, "The Middle Path, avoiding the extremes, gives vision and knowledge and leads to calm, realization, enlightenment, and Nibbâna."

It's why Einstein asserted, "Science without religion is lame, religion without science is blind."

It's why Admiral James Stockdale told his men that "facing the brutal facts" while at the same time "holding on to the faith that you will eventually prevail" was the secret of keeping hope alive during the horrors of the Hanoi Hilton.

It's why Mary Kay Ash made millions by helping women advance their careers while still nurturing their families.

It's why Barack Obama inspired a nation of previously apathetic voters when he proclaimed, "We're not a red America or a blue America, we're the United States of America."

It's why Elvis Presley was able to shake, rattle, and roll his way to a hundred and fifty gold records, when white kids and black kids took the floor and danced like nobody was watching.

I've used the Triangle of Truth to facilitate between warring departments in the Fortune 500 and to help entrepreneurs innovate on minimal budgets, and I've also used it to create more love and intimacy within my own family.

If there's one thing I've found to be true in all those situations, it's this: We humans say we want to change, but what we really want is for everybody else to change first. The Triangle of Truth solves that problem. It enables people, departments, churches, and even nations to all change at the same time. It allows you to see another

> We humans say we want to change, but what we really want is for everybody else to change first.

person's perspective, while at the same time giving you a language for helping them to see yours.

The ability to assimilate what often seem to be two conflicting points of view isn't easy. Our need to be right and our fear of not getting what we want often hold us back from creating the solutions we so desperately need and crave. But learning to discern and honor the truth of another is always worth the effort. Because at the end of the day, we all want the same thing—we just want to be happy.

The Triangle of Truth can help you find the happiness that you deserve, and it will help you create more success along the way. Whether you're worried about love, money, your in-laws, your kids, or the prospects for world peace, trust me, the answers are closer than you know. Whatever hurt you're carrying in your heart right now, I promise you, it can be healed. And whatever conflict you're facing, it can be solved.

We're at a crossroads on this planet, both within ourselves and with our systems. We're searching for a way to make our outer world match the inner yearnings of our hearts. It's a challenging process, but it can be done. It can be done by you, and it can be done by me, and it can be done by everyone who believes that we deserve something more than fighting, stress, and angst.

You see, you have a larger purpose in this world. We all do. You weren't sent here to be unhappy, broke, or sleep deprived. And you certainly weren't sent here to spend all your time frustrated with other people. Quite simply, you were sent here to love and be loved, and you were meant to make a meaningful contribution during your stay on Earth.

I want to help you find an easier way to do that. I want you to experience more peace, love, and joy while you're on this planet, and I want you to see how much your time here truly matters.

Nobody deserves love and happiness more than you do.

Embrace *And*

Why Either/Or Thinking Ruins Everything

In all intellectual debates both sides
tend to be correct in what they affirm and
wrong in what they deny.
—John Stuart Mill

It usually comes down to the speeches.

You know, the ones you rehearse in your head for when you finally get to tell so-and-so what you *really* think about them.

Your monologue gets more brilliant each day as you practice it in your shower or car. Clarifying your thoughts, honing your points, prepping for the day when at last you take the filters off and let them have it.

The stunning clarity and accuracy with which you deliver your soliloquy will be amazing. In fact, they will probably be rendered absolutely speechless, because as we all know, there is no defense against the truth—the real truth, that is.

And that's what you're going to confront them with. The truth.

The truth about how they're blind to any opinion except their own.

Or perhaps it's the truth about the way they twist around the facts and manipulate others into taking their side.

Or maybe they're always emotionally absent, ignoring the people who need them and not even caring how much it hurts.

Or a chronic liar who gets their way by scheming and cheating.

Or perhaps they're a perpetual victim, blaming everyone else for their problems and never taking responsibility for their own self-created mess.

Or a passive-aggressive type who acts nice in public and secretly sabotages people behind their backs.

Or a whiner, who complains about everything, and sucks the life out of everyone.

Or maybe they're just plain nasty and negative and you're tired of dealing with it.

Yes sir, it will be a fine moment indeed when you finally confront them. Because once you speak the truth, there can be no more denials. No more manipulating, no more game-playing, no more falsehoods, and no more lies.

The jig is up.

You're wise to their wicked ways and you're not going to let them get away with this behavior any longer.

We've all been there. Dreaming about how satisfying it would feel to call so-and-so on the carpet. Picturing the slack-jawed look on their face when they realize that they've been caught.

It's a fantasy you can practically taste. Whether it's the crazy sister-in-law, the negative coworker, or the selfish spouse, there's nothing like the dysfunctions of others to bring out the beast in us.

Why Other People Drive Us Nuts

What makes us even more crazy is the way they always seem to get away with it. It's almost like nobody but us can see the real truth. If other people do see it, they're not willing to do anything about it.

So we create the speeches, savoring the righteousness of our words as we turn them over and over again in our mind, envisioning the moment when justice is served and we expose the offender for who and what they really are.

The evil boss will be fired and have to do the walk of shame to the parking lot as the HR director escorts him to his car.

The family will finally tell the drama queen sister-in-law that they're no longer going to put up with her antics.

The nasty coworker will be called on the carpet for derailing projects and leaking their venom all over the office.

And the opinionated neighbor will be exposed as the self-serving, ill-informed, narrow-minded person that they are.

Once the truth is on the table, people can no longer pretend to be something that they're not. Others will finally know exactly what category of person they are.

This is important, because life is a lot easier to understand when people are categorized. In fact, there's nothing the human mind likes better than putting people into categories.

Good, bad, smart, dumb, helpful, hurtful, kind, manipulative.

You're either acting right or you're acting wrong, and once we decide that you're one thing, we're often quite reluctant to consider the notion that you may be something else.

You're either this, or that.

Therein lies the problem.

Our minds prefer the simplicity of either/or. But until we're willing to embrace the possibility of *And*, we're doomed to keep repeating the same conflicts over and over and over again.

The Flawed *And* Fabulous Dichotomy of Human Nature

Nothing reveals the human tendency toward either/or thinking more than the judgments we cast on other people.

Here's how it usually works.

Someone says or does something that we don't agree with—be it a hurtful spouse, annoying in-law, manipulative boss, or ill-informed political adversary—we label their behavior as bad, and our negative perception of them becomes the primary lens through which we view their every action. With our negative filter in place, we then either ignore any good qualities they may have or we minimize them, telling ourselves why their bad behavior overshadows everything else.

> **Until we're willing to embrace the possibility of *And*, we're doomed to keep repeating the same conflicts over and over and over again.**

You've probably seen this dynamic play out with people who can't stop talking about how awful their ex-spouse is. The marriage may be over, but until the world recognizes just how badly their ex did them wrong, they can't let it go. Everything their ex-spouse says or does further proves their awfulness. It's an either/or game, and if one person is the good guy the other person must be the bad guy.

But how many of us haven't done the same thing ourselves (albeit in perhaps less obvious or dramatic ways)? I know that I've certainly been guilty of writing people off after they do something I think is wrong. Once you get a negative take on someone, it becomes hard for you to assimilate any good information about them into your brain.

For example, if you find out that someone is a Republican or a Democrat, how does that affect your perception of them? If you're like most of us, if they're the same party you are, you'll likely to be pleased. But the second you find out that they're one of the other guys, you probably tend to discount much of what they say, even if they're not talking about politics.

We don't just label individuals; we also do it with entire groups of people. History is fraught with examples of how either/or labeling has resulted in wars, prejudice, and political stalemates that last for centuries. Our tendency to categorize people as either good or bad wreaks havoc on our personal relationships, undermines our organizations, and creates problems for us everywhere we go.

Which is kind of ironic. While most of us will readily admit that we ourselves are a combination of both good and bad, we have a hard time accepting this duality in others. It's almost as if our brains can't assimilate the idea that other people might be just as flawed and fabulous as we are.

As in your nutty relatives might be both manipulative *and* kind.

Your evil boss may be self-serving *and* want the best for the company.

And your spouse may be self-absorbed *and* also love you more than you can possibly imagine.

The truth is, we're all flawed. We're also all fabulous, and while our dysfunctions may camouflage our magnificence, they don't negate it.

So what does this have to do with Buddha, Mary Kay, the Triangle of Truth, and helping you create a lifetime of happiness and love?

Everything.

Either/Or: The Bane of Human Existence

When I first started this project, I wanted to answer two simple questions.

Why do we drive each other crazy, and how can we create peace?

After spending the better part of two decades coaching executives, arguing about politics, training thousands of salespeople, running leadership seminars, succeeding and failing in business, raising a family, and trying to stay happily married to someone of the opposite sex, *opposite* being the operative word here, I've come to realize that the way we relate to each other is the foundation for everything we do. When we stay stuck in conflict and strife, we fail. When we create positive connections with others, we accomplish more than we ever could alone.

The trouble is, sometimes other people are so doggone annoying that, more often than not, they seem to be causing us problems rather than helping us solve them.

On a surface level it often seems like we have lots of problems. Our family drives us crazy, relationships continue to disappoint, the people at work don't act the way we think they should, and when it comes to politics and religion, half the world usually seems just plain nuts.

However if you look beneath our frustrations with others, you'll almost always find an either/or style of thinking, on one or both sides. It's a mind-set that often keeps us stuck in the problems, rather than creating a solution.

We might like to believe that the challenges that we face at work are different from problems we face at home, and that what's going on in the world is different from what's happening inside our own relationships, but the common denominator in all those situations is us, and the way that we think.

The way that we think affects every facet of our lives, and when we get stuck in the either/or mind-set, it spills out into everything that we do.

The human tendency to put people into categories reflects an either/or style of thinking that stymies not only our relationships, but also everything else. Either/or labeling, be it of people or ideas, closes our mind to new information. Which in turn prevents us from seeing the big picture, and keeps us from creating anything different than what we've already got.

The very same either/or thinking that prompts people to label their neighbors or in-laws as judgmental nuts is the exact either/or thinking that causes problems at work, in love, and in life. In most cases it's not the situation, it's the thought pattern.

And while either/or thinking is easy to spot in others, it's often harder to recognize in ourselves. But you know all those annoying people who can't seem to see any perspective other than their own?

> While either/or thinking is easy to spot in others, it's often harder to recognize in ourselves.

Well, unfortunately, when we become frustrated with *their* one-dimensional thinking, we often start to do the exact same thing ourselves. It doesn't really matter who starts it; once we descend into an either/or mind-set, we lose the ability to solve our problems because all creative thinking stops.

But if you can learn to lift your mind out of either/or, you will literally become smarter about everything.

That's why this book isn't about relationships, business, politics, or religion. It's about all those things, because until we get smarter about the way we approach each other and our potential conflicts, our lives can't really get any better.

Harnessing the Power of *And*

I've spent the last several years unraveling the age-old problem of why we make each other nuts, and after dissecting hundreds of business conflicts, personal squabbles, and even holy wars, an interesting pattern emerged.

The world is filled with dichotomies—men versus women, Right versus Left, freedom versus responsibility, nurture versus nature, strategic versus tactical—things that when pitted against each other cause conflict, yet when harnessed together create great results.

Our natural inclination is to try to rid ourselves of these dualities because we believe they cause conflict and strife.

Nothing could be further from the truth. Our conflicts don't hold us back; quite the opposite, they are, in fact, the secret to solving our problems. Success is not found in ignoring or compromising our dualities, but in learning to leverage them.

Success is not found in ignoring or compromising our dualities, but in learning to leverage them.

The ability to assimilate seemingly conflicting perspectives has been the invisible underpinning behind most of our great advances, public and private.

- ► Charles Darwin's *Origin of Species* was greatly improved by his devoutly religious wife, Emma, who served as his original editor. Emma's religious beliefs prompted Charles to more thoroughly research his then controversial theory of evolution, resulting in a much more complete offering rather than simply a diatribe against traditional religious teachings.

- ► The Third Way, a nonpartisan think tank founded in 2005, has become a go-to source for elected officials, candidates, and advocates seeking to advance moderate yet progressive policy ideas. Their issues trainings have been utilized extensively in the House and Senate, and their motto "come let us reason together to end the culture wars" transcends right-wing and left-wing ideologies.

► Dr. Christiane Northrup became the guru of women's health and has penned four bestsellers because she was one of the first mainstream doctors to combine cutting-edge science with time-honored spiritual wisdom.

Combining multiple disciplines improves our organizations:

► A savvy corporate VP I once coached doubled her market share when she decided to quit playing mediator between her warring department heads. Instead of trying to coerce a compromise, she made a proactive choice to leverage their differing perspectives. She ended the turf wars and created a record-breaking organization in which every single person was aligned toward the big picture goal.

► A large industrial client of mine implemented a rigorous national safety program while at the same time increasing their per man-hour productivity, shocking the competition as well as many of their own employees, who had always assumed that safety slowed people down.

Assimilating multiple perspectives also improves the way we love:

► Parenting expert Amy McCready, founder of Positive

Parenting Solutions, built a business around teaching parents how to provide their kids with structure and freedom at the same time. Parents in her classes are frequently moved to tears when they discover that they don't have to choose between playing the heavy and being a compassionate parent.

► Relationship guru Harville Hendrix, author of *Getting the Love You Want*, transforms relationships by showing couples how their inherent differences actually provide a path for mutual growth, rather than anger, angst, and sorrow. Decade-long grievances evaporate in a single session when both perspectives are finally heard and honored.

Where others saw only either/or, these visionary thinkers harnessed the power of *And*. Their ability to assimilate seemingly competing concepts, ideas, and disciplines enabled them to solve problems that others had deemed unsolvable.

Yet in each of these situations, either/or thinking didn't die an easy death:

► People are still arguing about Darwin's theory of evolution 150 years after he wrote it.

► Politicians remain trapped in Right versus Left battles, and many are provoking culture wars, rather than trying to end them.

► Western medicine has been slow to embrace the spiritual elements of healing, and many doctors still dismiss anything other than Western science.

▸ My VP client had to waste hours of precious time coddling people before they finally felt secure enough to quit undermining their colleagues and recognize that they were all on the same team.

▸ Many managers at the industrial company initially resisted the additional safety measures, believing they were overkill that would interfere with their productivity goals.

▸ Parenting expert McCready has to spend the better part of every class reassuring uneasy parents that adding discipline or freedom to their parenting repertoire doesn't have to mean giving up either one.

▸ "Getting the Love You Want" workshop instructors routinely encounter participants whose marriages are in the ditch, yet who still stubbornly cling to the idea that their version of the problems is the only one that's accurate.

It's easy to say that we want to combine perspectives, but when emotions and egos are involved, it's often not as simple as we would like.

Intellectually Understandable, Emotionally Challenging

The Triangle of Truth model—the ability to hold two seemingly competing ideas in your mind at the same time and put them together in a way that makes their whole greater than the sum of their parts—makes sense from an intellectual perspective. The people who see both sides of the Triangle move to a higher level, while those who cling to one side remain stuck.

Here's where it get tricky. The model doesn't apply just to relationships, business, politics, and creative endeavors. It applies to individuals as well.

Just as there are dualities in the world, there are dualities within each of us. We can be selfish and we can be selfless. We can be disciplined and we can be lazy. We can be judgmental and we can be accepting. All at the same time.

The problem isn't that we have these dualities, it's that we don't see their value.

We beat each other up for the negative side of our personalities, without ever considering the possibility that our seemingly competing perspectives might actually work for our collective benefit.

Think about it: Do you honestly believe the world would be a better place if everyone had the exact same strengths and weaknesses as you?

The beauty of the human tapestry is that what one of us lacks, the other one has. Whether it's divine intervention or a happy accident, annoying habits in one person can often push a button in someone else that gives them the impetus to grow.

However, human relationships are anything but logical, and when you throw stress and emotions into the mix, it's often hard for us to see the big picture.

I can be delighted as all get-out that men as a collective whole tend to be more linear and have stronger sex drives than women. But if I'm trying to scan my emails, supervise the kids, and cook dinner all at the same time, and my husband walks in the door, makes a beeline for me and gives me the "honey let's take a nap" shoulder rub, I'm going to feel less than delighted.

I may agree with the premise that my in-laws, coworkers, and neighbors have just as much right to take up space on this planet as I do. But the minute they start in with their "stuff," it becomes hard for me to see how they're adding much value to the human condition.

That's why the real power of the Triangle of Truth lies in our ability to take the model from the abstract—from the intellect—into the world of emotions.

The model itself, combining opposites for a great whole, represents a shift in the way that we traditionally think and feel about other people and the way that we think and feel about ourselves.

The reason we drive each other nuts is the very same reason that we struggle to solve our business, parenting, political, and community challenges. It's because we're usually unable to see any perspective beyond our own. We're uncomfortable with the potential uncertainty of combining our views for a bigger *And*. So our minds take the easy route, filling in the blanks to convince us that everything is either/or. And the world proceeds accordingly as we argue, bicker, and fight over who's right and who's wrong.

> **The real power of the Triangle of Truth lies in our ability to take the model from the world of the abstract into the world of emotions.**

Why a Single Triangle Solves
Millions of Problems

Scientists say that for a theory to be proven valid, it must pass the test of parsimony. The easier the theory is to understand and the more things it explains, the more parsimonious it is. Rooted in the Latin word *parsimonia*, or "to spare," parsimony is defined as "less is better."

Newton's law of gravity passes the test of parsimony. It's easy to understand (stuff falls toward the center of the earth), and it applies to everything from apples to feathers to the human body. You can apply it again and again, to any matter, in any setting, anywhere in the world, and it will always hold true.

Darwin's theory of evolution also passes the parsimony test. It's elegantly simple—species evolve over time via natural selection—and it explains everything from why cockroaches have crunchy shells to why babies smile. It all goes back to survival of the fittest.

Darwin once said, "In scientific investigations, it is permitted to invent any hypothesis and, if it explains various large and independent classes of facts, it rises to the rank of a well-grounded theory."

The Triangle of Truth is a well-grounded theory. It has been tested on everything from business battles to church conflicts to toilet seat wars, and while it might not be in the Newton or Darwin category, it does indeed pass the test of parsimony.

The common thread inside every disagreement, be it a global conflict or two individuals bickering about the best way to load a dishwasher, is either/or thinking, a belief on both sides that we're right, so therefore, the other side must be wrong.

The nurture versus nature debate, male versus female conflicts, forest versus trees quagmires, and the evolution versus creationism argument all continue to rage because neither side is willing to acknowledge any truth on the other side.

> Compromise isn't sustainable over the long haul because it requires us to water down our truths when in reality we should be bringing them together.

Traditional compromise doesn't work, any more than throwing an apple in the sky and expecting it to stay there would. Compromise isn't sustainable over the long haul because it requires us to water down our truths when in reality we should be bringing them together.

The Triangle of Truth is a model for bringing our truths together. When you make a conscious effort to use it, things become more civilized, and people are less defensive and angry.

However, if you use it with the sole intent of trying to get your way and make other people see your side, you won't be tapping into its full power.

If you truly want to solve problems and change situations for the better, you have to go beyond using the model with others. You have to be willing to apply it yourself.

The Triangle of Truth only works as well externally as you're willing to apply it internally. It's hard to change the way other people think, until you change the way *you* think.

Said another way, you can't have peace with others until you create peace within.

That's why you have to be willing to get out of your head and into your heart. While you may be able to articulate all the intellectual reasons why you're in the right, unless you soften your heart to others, you will continue to find yourself embroiled in either/or debates, even if only in your own mind.

The Triangle of Truth only works as well externally as you're willing to apply it internally.

Which circles us right back to our frustrations with the button-pushing relatives, negative coworkers, and selfish significant others.

One of the reasons that we get so frustrated with them is that it feels like they're living a lie—out there acting all nice and normal for the rest of the world, when we know what they're *really* like. We want to expose the truth, or at least the truth the way we see it.

But fantasizing about exposing the misdeeds of others never makes for a very fine life, or at least it doesn't feel like one to me. Neither does practicing little speeches in my car, or lying awake at night stewing about how so-and-so did me wrong, or ruminating about how great it would be to call them out.

I've wasted a lot of my precious time on this earth doing all those things, and I can't see that it really got me anywhere. It's nice to be right, and trust me I often am, as I'm sure you are as well. Yet as the common expression goes: Do you want to be right or happy?

With the Triangle of Truth, you don't have to choose. You can be right and happy at the same time. You don't have to give up your assessments of other people. The Triangle of Truth simply opens up a space for you to add additional information.

You can be right and happy at the same time.

Once you start using the model with the people who are driving you nuts, you'll find that it creates a mental shift that resonates out onto every other area of your life. When you make a conscious decision to lift yourself out of either/or thinking, you are literally retraining your brain.

Filed Under Flawed

We don't judge and categorize people because we've evil. We judge and categorize people because that's what our minds were meant to do. The human brain is really just one big giant categorizing machine.

We can't possibly stop to ponder the millions of things we encounter each day. So we categorize them, deciding instantaneously whether something is this or that. Good, bad; fruit, vegetable; sports car, salad dressing. It's the way we make sense of the world.

Your brain can't tolerate a bunch of random objects just floating around out there; your mind has to put them somewhere. So we create little mental file folders, and once the categorizing machine puts something into one file, it's hard to convince us that it belongs anywhere else.

Just try getting your mind to accept the idea that a car should be moved into the salad dressing category and you'll see that your brain won't cooperate. It almost screams, "It's not salad dressing, it's an automobile. You drive it, you don't pour it over leafy greens."

And should anyone try to tell you differently, you would rightly think they're nuts.

Because you know the truth. You've seen the evidence. A car is transportation; it's not food. Yes, technically you can drive and eat at the same time, but cars and food are housed in two separate mental file folders and your brain will work overtime to prove that it has them in the right spots.

It's a basic human instinct, and it serves us well much of the time.

However, our either/or sorting system limits us when we apply it to other people. Once we uncover a truth about someone— they're selfish, they lied, their politics are self-serving—we tend to label their file folder and slam it shut. Case closed. We've seen the evidence, and our mind has put them in the appropriate slot. We're not going to dig out their folder and relabel it.

It's almost as if our brains are operating like a 1980s hierarchical computer. The kind of system where each file can only be stored in one place.

However, by consciously reframing things, we can rise above the limitations of our oh-so-human either/or instincts. The Triangle of Truth provides a more creative platform. It allows you to put your mother-in-law in the dysfunctional folder, and also in the "wants the best for her family" file.

As opposed to hard file folders, where things get locked in place, the Triangle of Truth encourages more fluidity and expansiveness in your thinking.

If you've seen firsthand evidence that someone is selfish, or underhanded, or possessing of some other not so pleasant quality, your mind isn't going to let go of that information. The Triangle of Truth provides you with a place to put that data, so that you can then add to it with additional information. It's a way to avoid staying stuck on one side of the line, furiously defending the single truth your brain wants to hold on to.

By providing a mental placeholder for your most important thoughts and values on one side of the Triangle, you can literally unlock your brain to see the other side. And that single mental shift changes everything.

The Truth About Other People

The truth is, other people are flawed; they're badly flawed.

They're selfish, they're mean, they're cheap, they're sloppy, they're lazy, and in most cases they're completely unwilling to even acknowledge that they're doing anything wrong. No matter how many times we point it out to them.

People are hopelessly flawed. They always were, and they probably always will be.

The only real hope we have for creating peace is to start seeing people for who they really are, both the good and the bad, and to not let their flaws keep us from enjoying them.

Oh, I know all the excuses, and I've offered them up many times myself.

But, you don't know my in-laws, they're awful. And the guy who

> The only real hope we have for creating peace is for us to start seeing people for who they really are, both the good and the bad.

cheated me on that business deal, he can never be forgiven, that was my life savings. As for my spouse, well, you have no idea how much he or she has hurt me.

I've been there, and I have no doubt that you've been wronged. I'm not suggesting you put up with mistreatment. But at a certain point we're going to have to get over ourselves and make peace with the fact that other people are dysfunctional. If we want to have any relationships in our life at all, we're going to have to start seeing some of their redeeming qualities or we'll drive ourselves nuts.

And we're going to have to admit that maybe we're not right about everything.

Because there's one person whose flawed and fabulous nature we haven't talked about yet, and that's yours.

It's true. You're probably just as flawed and fabulous as all the people you're frustrated with. The trouble is, as hard as it is to accept this duality in others, sometimes it's even harder to accept in ourselves.

We're usually either trying to pretend we're perfect or we're beating ourselves up because we're not. We're either trying to prove we're right, or we're terrified that we're wrong.

Let's be honest here; you know all that energy we spend rehearsing those little speeches? (And believe me, I've done my share of shower stall eloquence as well.)

It's not really about exposing the truth about how the other guy has done wrong, is it? It's about making sure that everyone knows the truth about how we've done right. All the drama we create around the misdeeds of others is really just our ego's way of justifying our own position.

But you can't make peace with the flawed and fabulous nature of others until you make peace with your own flawed and fabulous self.

That's why at its core, the Triangle of Truth is more than a problem-solving model or business tool; it's also a template for personal growth. It calls on you to embrace not only the best of people but also the worst; and to look with clear-eyed understanding at your own shortcomings, and to decide to love yourself anyway.

> **The Triangle of Truth is more than a problem-solving model or business tool; it's also a template for personal growth.**

We're never going to get rid of our flaws, any more than we're ever all going to agree on politics, religion, or sofa fabric.

But if we can make peace with the fact that we're all flawed, and we're also all fabulous, and that no one person is right about everything, things will start to change. Not just in our personal relationships, but in our businesses, our communities, and, lofty as it sounds, perhaps in the world.

When we acknowledge that both sides of the Triangle, the good and the bad, exist within each of us, we no longer have anything to prove, to ourselves or anyone else. The moment that we decide to redirect our energy away from attacking and defending is the very moment that we open up a space to create something better, both for ourselves and for others.

You can't create greatness if you're locked in the middle of either/or debates. And you won't find peace if your only goal is to get your way.

It is only by lifting our hearts and minds toward a larger vision that we can become who we were truly meant to be. Which is flawed and fabulous people who appreciate their fellow humans beings even when they're driving us nuts, because we understand that we're all just a work in progress and the best answers come from our combined points of view, even if the process of getting there is messy.

The ability to rise above either/or thinking is a challenging skill to master, especially in a world that so often encourages division and polarization. Yet if we can embrace the duality of *And*, we will literally lift our minds to a higher plane.

But in order to rise above the either/or debates that keep holding us back, someone has to be willing to use it first.

I'm hoping that person will be you.

Make Peace with Ambiguity

How Fear and Uncertainty Flatline Our Thinking

Neurosis is the inability to tolerate ambiguity.
—Sigmund Freud

When people first learn about the Triangle of Truth, their initial reaction is often, "That sounds great, and *I'm* certainly willing to see both sides of an issue, but I doubt I could get so-and-so to go along."

I'm going to let you in on a big secret: The Triangle of Truth works even when the other side refuses to play along.

They can stay just as narrow-minded and stubborn as ever. All it takes is for one person to start using the model and the energy will shift. The problem is, we're afraid.

Afraid that if we acknowledge their side, they won't acknowledge ours.

Afraid that if we try to meet their needs, we'll be giving up on our own.

Afraid that if we give them a forum for their agenda, ours will be forgotten.

Afraid that if we acknowledge what they're doing right, they'll never own up to what they're doing wrong.

Afraid that letting them have their way means that we can never get ours.

Why are so we afraid? Would it kill us to listen to their point of view, or to find some truth in what they're saying?

Actually there's a little part of our brain that believes that yes, it will kill us to see their side of things. It's a primitive part of your mind that doesn't know the difference between a threat to your life and a threat to your ego.

This Is Your Brain on Fear

Fear comes from our reptilian brain. It's a little part of your brain that sits right at the top of your spine, buried beneath the more emotional limbic brain, the logical neocortex, and the higher-minded frontal lobes. Scientists refer to it as the reptilian brain because it's a leftover from our prehistoric ancestors dating back five hundred million years and it resembles the brain structure of, well, a reptile.

Our reptilian brain operates on total instinct, and its primary purpose it to keep you alive. Picture a beady-eyed little lizard clutching a cracker crumb, darting his head from side to side, trying to protect his bounty, and you'll have a pretty clear picture of the reptilian brain. It sees danger at every turn, and while it's usually reliable, in the sense that it does what it's supposed to, scientists also note that it tends to be somewhat rigid and compulsive.

Sound like anyone you know?

Your reptilian brain doesn't care if you're happy; it just wants to keep you breathing. So it categorizes almost everything, and everyone, as a potential threat to your safety. It can't tell the difference between someone who cuts you off in traffic because they're late for work and not paying attention, versus someone who is trying to ram their car into you, steal your money, and eat your young.

They both feel like imminent danger.

Once the little lizardlike fear instinct kicks in, it can control the entire rest of your brain, without you even realizing it. Fear radiates out from your reptilian brain into the emotions of your limbic brain, the language and logic of your neocortex, and even the executive functions of decision making and purpose housed in your frontal lobes.

That's why when somebody cuts you off at an exit ramp, you get angry (emotion) and decide he's a jerk (logic), curse him under your breath (language), then reach the conclusion that the only way to make him pay for his mistake is to tailgate him or speed up next to him and give him the finger (decision making and purpose).

Are you getting what's happening here? A little fear-based lizard just hijacked the whole system, and it took less than two seconds.

But the face of fear doesn't always manifest itself as red-faced anger. Sometimes fear shows up looking quite sophisticated and smiling. Look behind the eyes of a slick-suited CEO using a twenty-seven-slide PowerPoint presentation to explain why the income statement isn't really reflective of how great the company is doing, so year-end bonuses should still be awarded in order to inspire another big year of hard to explain progress, and you'll see a scared little lizard clutching his cracker crumb with all his might.

Not that I'm above such behaviors myself. At one point in my life I was actually able to convince an entire sales force that putting the competitor out of business was a noble endeavor. Heck, I even designed an incentive plan around it.

When your brain is in the clutches of fear, it will employ every skill you've got to annihilate the perceived threat.

It doesn't matter if it's a real threat or just something that makes you a little bit uncomfortable. Sometimes all it takes is for someone to challenge your political affiliation or your parenting skills, and the lizard leaps into action.

While on the surface you may look like a sophisticated human being in control of your destiny; in reality, a little reptile is driving the bus. A little reptile who isn't smart enough to understand that not everyone is trying to take away his crumb. That's why when your mother-in-law criticizes the way you manage money, it feels like she is taking a gun to your head and forcing you to cough up your wallet. Or when your boss makes a snippy comment about things being disorganized, you take it personally and feel like he's publicly berating you in front of the entire staff.

Fear ignites the negative emotions, which causes your brain to create language and logic to justify the way you feel, and then you decide what action you want to take, based on the arguments you just created.

Remember the little speeches we create in our heads and our tendency to categorize people as good or bad?

That's your brain on fear.

The fear that someone might get away with bad behavior, or that someone else's agenda might take priority over our own, causes the lizard to leap into action. Your reptilian brain categorizes the person or idea as a threat, your limbic brain supplies the anger, then your neocortex creates a little speech to prove itself right, and your frontal lobes convince you that you're doing it for the benefit of others.

Kind of sad, isn't it?

It's all so primitive and predictable. Yet it happens every single day, and while it might keep us safe, at least in the short term, it sure doesn't make us happy.

The "I Can't Hear You" Brain-Lock

Fear (both real and imagined) keeps us stuck in either/or thinking. It prevents us from using the Triangle of Truth and harnessing the power of *And* because of what I refer to as the *brain-lock phenomenon.*

It's when our brain locks in on something we know to be true, and we expend every ounce of our energy defending it. So much so, that we are blind and deaf to any truth on the other side.

If you've ever watched a far right and far left commentator scream at each other on television, you've seen the brain-lock phenomenon in action. They might as well put their fingers in their ears, and shout, "I can't hear you, I can't hear you."

But the same thing happens to us at home, work, and even in the drive-through line.

Someone says something you disagree with, criticizes you, or does something that makes you feel uncomfortable. Your reptilian brain goes into fear mode, because, again, it can't tell the difference between a real threat and an imagined one.

With the reptilian brain transmitting fear, the rest of the brain locks in on any information that will help defend itself against the perceived threat. But your brain isn't stupid, at least the bigger part on top isn't, so it's not going to pick just any piece of information. It has to be true. Something like, he's hurt me in the past, she never has anything nice to say, or *my* politics are based on moral values.

However, as smart as your big brain may be, it's also under the influence of fear, and it's being controlled by the little reptile buried underneath. So it perceives pretty much anything as a threat, including additional information or opinions, which might require the whole system to rethink its original position— something it hates to do.

Your high-minded self might know that you don't have all the answers and that person sitting across from you is just as likely to be right as you are. But your little lizard brain isn't interested in collaborating with another flawed and fabulous human being. All the lizard brain knows is that this person is a threat that needs to be shut down.

And you find yourself frustrated and angry. Again.

That's why it's hard to use the Triangle of Truth when you're afraid. Because you brain locks down on what you know to be true, and expends all its energy defending your side of the Triangle. Shouting the truth over and over again—in your mind or out loud.

So how do you break the brain-lock?

It's quite simple.

Love.

People often think that courage is the opposite of fear. But that's not true at all. The opposite of fear is love. Love is what **Love is what fuels courage.**
fuels courage.

It has been said that there are
only two real emotions, love and fear, and that all our other emotions are derivatives of those. I agree. Love expands, while fear
contracts. The secret of quelling fear, even minor fear, is to harness the power of love.

It doesn't matter whether we're at work or at home, dealing
with someone we care about or a stranger. When we're in the
clutches of fear, we get defensive and angry, and we're more
likely to find fault. But when we make the decision to apply love,
our hearts and minds expand, and we're open to more creative
solutions.

Fear Ignites Either/Or, Love Inspires *And*

It might not seem like there's a connection between love and our
business, political, or organizational problems. And I'm certainly
not so naive as to think that joining hands around a campfire
and singing "Kumbaya" is going to fix Wall Street or create peace
in the Middle East.

It's not so much that love actually solves our conflicts and
problems, it's that it enables us to start the process. Because
when you make a conscious decision to move out of fear-based

thinking into love-based thinking you open yourself up to the possibility of *And*.

Fear prevents you from using the Triangle of Truth because it keeps you stuck on your side of the line defending your position, afraid that if you give an inch, they'll win.

Love enables you to calm down for a minute and see the other side. You don't have to love the person you're dealing with; you don't even have to like them. You just need to get yourself into a loving space in your own heart and mind, and that in and of itself will change your thinking, which is sometimes all you need to create a different dynamic.

However, one of the problems with fear is that we frequently don't recognize it when we're experiencing it, because it often masquerades as other more socially acceptable qualities, like competitiveness, pride, and sometimes even responsibility and maturity. We often convince ourselves that we're doing the right thing, when really we're just afraid of something else. Like the person who convinces themselves that being a workaholic is a responsible way to take care of their family, but in reality they're deathly afraid of intimacy. (Ouch!)

Rather than risking a potentially uncomfortable situation, our mind tells us that our thinking is correct, and that our way is the right way, in fact it's the only way, or at least the only sensible way. We're too afraid to consider something different, so we descend into the default of either/or.

The way you can tell the difference between fear and love is how you feel in your gut. Fear creates tension, whereas love creates ease. When you're in a place of fear, you're always ready to defend your side. But when you're in a place of love, you're more open.

People often think of love as a soft emotion, or something that we reserve for our personal rela- tionships. That's also not the case.

Love is patient, love is kind, and all those other nicey-nice things ministers like to remind us about at weddings. Love is

Love is also the single most powerful force on this planet.

also the single most powerful force on this planet.

Love has been the cornerstone of every successful endeavor since the dawn of time. From the American Revolution to Apple Computer, great countries, great companies, great com- munities, and great families have all been fueled by people who showed up with love. People who put their heart and soul into what they were doing, and who would do just about anything for the people they cared about. Love is what enables people to put aside their own ego on behalf of something bigger than themselves.

Love is one of the secrets of making the Triangle of Truth work; it puts it on turbocharge. Making the decision to show up with love means making a decision to rise above your own perspec- tive and consider the big picture.

Think about it. If you go into a meeting determined to get your way, it's highly likely that you'll succumb to either/or think- ing the first time your own agenda feels threatened.

But if you go into that same meeting, thinking about how you can show more love to your customers, your employees, or your coworkers, you're going to be more open.

When you come from a place of fear you're coming from a

place of ego, which tends to makes you defensive and almost always prompts a defensive reaction in others. When you make the decision to choose love, be it love for your country, love for your family, love for your work, or even just love of life, you care more about solving the problems than you do about trying to prove yourself right.

Fear is about trying to get your way right now. Love is about being patient enough to put your thoughts and ideas on pause and consider the big picture.

Love is more powerful than fear, because when you come from a place of love, you bring more than just your mind into situations; you also bring your heart. Your heart is connected to your soul, which is where your real power lies.

While your mind may prefer the simplicity of either/or, and want everything settled right now, your soul is yearning for something bigger. Your mind wants to be right, but your soul wants to make a difference.

> **Your mind wants to be right, but your soul wants to make a difference.**

Your soul doesn't care about getting the biggest budget, proving your in-laws wrong, or winning a political battle of wits. The deepest yearning of your soul is to be peaceful and happy, and the best part of you also wants other people to be peaceful and happy as well.

When you choose love, you tap into the wisdom of your soul. Love enables you to rise above either/or thinking because it helps you calm your mind. When you're calm, you're more able to tolerate uncertainty.

So let's go ahead and dismiss the notion that love makes you weak. Love makes you stronger, and it's more powerful than fear any day of the week.

Love isn't for wimps, it's for heroes. There's no one who demonstrates that better than Admiral James Stockdale.

Love Lessons from the Hanoi Hilton

Admiral Stockdale was the highest-ranking officer in the Hanoi Hilton during the Vietnam era and became one of the most highly decorated officers in the U.S. Navy. He passed away with Alzheimer's at the age of eighty-one in 2005.

During his seven and half years of imprisonment at Hoa Lo prison, Stockdale was tortured over twenty times, routinely beaten, and spent much of his time locked in leg irons in a small bath stall. Yet with no prisoners' rights, no set release date, and no idea when or if he would ever see his family again, Stockdale shouldered the burden of command and is credited with creating the conditions that enabled his men to survive, unbroken.

Some may recall Stockdale's less than stellar debate performance as Ross Perot's vice presidential running mate in the 1992 election, when the crusty almost-seventy-year-old Navy veteran was thrown in the ring with more prepared professional politicians Al Gore and Dan Quayle. If you didn't know Stockdale's history, it was easy to allow either/or instincts to categorize him as ineffective based on this one isolated event.

However, the men who served with Stockdale, and the families whose husbands and fathers he saved, know that he is a true hero in every sense of the word.

Author Jim Collins describes Stockdale's moving story in his bestselling book *Good to Great*:

> *At one point he beat himself with a stool and cut himself with a razor, deliberately disfiguring himself so that he could not be put on videotape as an example of a "well-treated prisoner."*
>
> *He exchanged secret intelligence information with his wife, knowing that discovery would mean more torture and perhaps death. He instituted rules that would help people deal with torture (no one can resist torture indefinitely, so he created a step-wise system—after x minutes, you can say certain things—that gave the men milestones to survive toward). He instituted an elaborate internal communications system to reduce the sense of isolation that their captors tried to create, which used a five-by-five matrix of tap codes for alphabet characters (tap-tap equals the letter a, tap-pause-tap-pause equals the letter b, tap-tap-pause equals the letter f, and so forth for twenty-five letters, with c doubling for k).*

Collins had the opportunity to meet with Stockdale while he and his team were researching *Good to Great*. The meeting had nothing to do with Collins's business book, or so he thought. One of Collins's students had written a paper on Stockdale, who at that time happened to be a research fellow studying Stoic philosophers at the Hoover Institution directly across the street from Collins's office. So Stockdale invited Collins and his student for lunch.

Collins prepared for the meeting by reading Stockdale's book *In Love and War*, written in alternating chapters by Stockdale and his wife, Sybil, chronicling their experiences during his seven and a half year imprisonment.

As Collins read the book he was struck by how depressing the story was. He knew the ending. Stockdale got out, reunited with his family, became a hero, and spent his later years studying philosophy on the beautiful Stanford campus. Yet how, Collins wondered, was Stockdale able to hold on to hope under horrific conditions when he didn't know his future fate? So he asked him as they walked to lunch.

"I never lost faith in the end of the story," Stockdale said. "I never doubted not only that I would get out, but also that I would prevail in the end and turn the experience into the defining event of my life, which in retrospect, I would not trade."

Collins didn't say anything for a few minutes as they continued their slow walk toward the faculty club, Stockdale limping and arc-swinging his stiff leg that had never fully recovered from repeated torture. Finally after about a hundred meters of silence Collins asked, "Who didn't make it out?"

"Oh, that's easy," he said. "The optimists."

"The optimists? I don't understand," said Collins, now completely confused, given what Stockdale had said earlier.

"The optimists. Oh, they were the ones who said, 'We're going to be out by Christmas.' And Christmas would come and Christmas would go. Then they'd say, 'We're going to be out by Easter' and Easter would come, and Easter would go. And then Thanksgiving, and then it would be Christmas again. And they died of a broken heart."

Another long pause, and more walking. Then he turned to Collins and said, "This is a very important lesson. You must never confuse faith that you will prevail in the end with the discipline to confront the most brutal facts of your current reality, whatever they may be."

Stockdale's story stayed with Collins. In *Good to Great* he cites the Stockdale Paradox—"the ability to retain the faith that you will prevail in the end, regardless of difficulties *And* at the same time confronting the most brutal facts of your current reality, whatever they might be, as a signature of those who create greatness, in their own lives or in leading others."

It's easy to see the Triangle of Truth in Stockdale's story: the ability to assimilate the brutal facts *and* hold on to the faith that you will prevail. Fact and faith are two concepts that often seem in conflict, yet Stockdale was able to combine them for the greater good of everyone.

I originally read Stockdale's story in *Good to Great*, and although I never had the chance to meet Stockdale himself, his story had a profound impact on me, both professionally and personally.

The image of this courageous man surviving torture, while holding on to the faith that he would prevail, has seen me through some pretty tough times. It's made me a better leader, and a better mother and wife. His courage in the face of horrific conditions has enabled me to face up to business and personal failures with dignity, honor, and hope. I've tried to emulate his example, and I've shared his story with every executive I've ever coached. I'm forever grateful to Jim Collins and his team. They not only wrote the best business book I've read, but they also had the insight to spot what has been for me a transformational life lesson.

Yet when I revisited Stockdale's story to write this book, I saw even more clearly how love fueled his every action.

At one point during their captivity, the prisoners were under an imposed silence, a practice frequently instituted by the jailers with the intent of isolating the POWs and breaking their bond. The men wanted to send a message to Stockdale, who was being held in isolation, so they took mops and brooms and swept the yard, slowly and deliberately tapping out a simple missive for their leader on the third anniversary of his being shot down.

Their message?

"We love you."

Not "You can do it" or "Keep your chin up" or even "Have courage," but "We love you."

The men instinctively knew that if they expressed their love for the leader, he would have the courage to go on. Their desire to express their love for Stockdale, even at the risk of discovery, was no doubt the result of the immeasurable love he had continually demonstrated for them.

Love gives us courage to hold on to faith, even when the facts are, as in Stockdale's case, as brutal as brutal can be.

Stockdale loved his men too much to lie. He wasn't going to humor them by telling them they were getting out by Christmas, because he knew in all likelihood that they weren't. He owed them the truth. But he also had faith that they would get out one day, and he kept reminding them of that truth as well.

He didn't allow the optimists to live on false hope or the pessimists to succumb to despair. He combined truths, facing the worst of the worst, while at the same time maintaining faith in the best of the best.

Pessimism Versus Optimism:
A False Choice

There are many situations where we find ourselves torn between pessimism and optimism. Although most of us will never face situations as horrific as Stockdale did, there will certainly be times in our lives when we will be called on to do our best in difficult situations.

The challenge is to avoid getting stuck in either doom and gloom pessimism or ill-informed optimism. One of the things I've observed during my years as a business consultant is that in many organizations, the pessimists and optimists are often at odds. There's usually one group of people who tend to be more predisposed to look at the facts, and they are inclined to say, "We're doomed, it's hopeless." But there's usually another set of people, in the same organization, facing the exact same situation, who are more inclined to say, "It's going to be OK, things will turn around."

Unfortunately, what frequently happens is that the pessimists become exasperated with the optimists because they think they're ignoring the facts. At the same time the optimists get equally frustrated with the pessimists, and accuse them of being a bunch Eeyores who suck the life out of everything.

The same thing happens in marriages. One person is shouting, "You're ignoring the facts," while the other person is screaming, "Why are you always so negative?"

Most of us are more predisposed to one side or the other; personally I think we're probably born that way. Perhaps it's part of a divine plan to make sure that the optimists don't go off half-cocked and the pessimists don't throw a wet blanket on every new idea. Or maybe it's just another quirk of human nature. Whatever the case, the earth and most organizations tend to be sprinkled with an assortment of both types, and they're frequently at odds.

But as Stockdale's story demonstrates, pessimism versus optimism is actually a false choice. The real duality we need to assimilate is fact and faith. If you love your family, your business, or your country, it's irresponsible to ignore the facts, even when they're ugly. In fact, especially when they're ugly. You can't solve a problem or create better systems without a firm grasp of what's going wrong now.

Yet when times are challenging, you also owe it to yourself, and to the people or cause that you care about, to never let go of the faith that you can and will prevail, even though you may not know exactly how or when.

Admiral Stockdale didn't know the end of the story, yet he faced the brutal facts with faith. I'm sure there were moments when he was afraid. But by consistently and consciously choosing love over fear, Stockdale was able to hold two seemingly incompatible truths—a horrific present and a hopeful future—in his mind at the same time.

It's the ultimate lesson in being able to tolerate ambiguity.

However, there's also another hero in the Stockdale story. This person didn't win the Congressional Medal of Honor or have a battleship named after her. But the love that she demonstrated in the face of uncertainty was no less courageous.

While Jim Stockdale was helping his men survive torture, unbeknownst to him, his wife Sybil was back in the States organizing the wives of servicemen who were in similar circumstances to form the League of American Families of POWs and MIAs.

With her husband's fate uncertain, Sybil Stockdale went to Washington to meet with the secretary of defense, calling for the president and Congress to publicly acknowledge the mistreatment of the POWs, something that they had never done even though they had evidence of gross mistreatment.

Sybil Stockdale believed that if more people knew about the mistreatment they would force the government to act. She personally made her group's demands known at the Paris Peace Talks, where private comments made to her by the head of the Vietnamese delegation revealed that they were afraid that her organization might catch the attention of the American public, something the North Vietnamese knew could turn the tide against them.

Mrs. Stockdale's group did capture public attention, the tide did turn, and eventually her husband was released, thanks in part to the efforts of his wife, and many other women who courageously stepped into leadership during a time when speaking up wasn't exactly proper service wife protocol. By confronting the facts and holding on to their faith, a group of military wives took on the U.S. secretary of defense and the North Vietnamese government.

Sybil Stockdale ultimately received the Navy's Distinguished Public Service Award, becoming the only wife of an active duty Naval officer to receive the award.

I share Sybil Stockdale's story because it demonstrates how love can fuel courage of many types and why choosing love enables us to rise up and be our best selves, even in the face of uncertainty.

I can't say that I've ever been as courageous as either of the Stockdales, but their example has certainly given me something to shoot for.

A few people suggested that I not use Admiral Stockdale in this book because of the poor impression he made during his ill-fated TV appearance in the vice presidential debates, an appearance that was lampooned on *Saturday Night Live* and from which his reputation never fully recovered. During a 1999 interview with Jim Lehrer, Stockdale said:

> *It was terribly frustrating because I remember I started with, "Who am I? Why am I here?" and I never got back to that because there was never an opportunity for me to explain my life to people. It was so different from Quayle and Gore. The four years in solitary confinement in Vietnam, seven and a half years in prisons, dropped the first bomb that started the first American bombing raid into North Vietnam. We blew the oil storage tanks off the map. And I never—I couldn't approach—I don't say it just to brag, but, I mean, my sensitivities are completely different.*

He was different, and that's precisely why I wanted to use his story. He and his wife are the kind of heroes I'd like to encounter more of. They were big thinkers who were able to rise above fear in the face of uncertainty. Their triumphs demonstrate how choosing love over fear enables us to harness the power of *And*, assimilating the duality of facts *And* faith, no matter how brutal our circumstances.

The judgments that many people cast upon Admiral Stockdale after his debate performance are a glaring example of how our default either/or instincts can prevent us from the seeing the full story of our fellow human beings. How often do we miss a miraculous person standing right in front of us because we've judged them after seeing only one side of their nature?

What POWs Teach Us About Choosing Our Thoughts

It is often during our most trying times that we gain the biggest insight into human nature.

Admiral Stockdale's story is not the only POW experience that gives us a lesson in choosing our response to bad situations. Just as we can learn lessons from people who do survive overwhelming odds, so too can we learn lessons from the unfortunate experiences of those who don't.

Donald Clifton, considered to be the grandfather of Positive Psychology, was inspired to spend his lifetime teaching people about the effects of positive emotions after reviewing a case study of how extreme psychological negativity affected American POWs during the Korean War.

The study, originally conducted by Major (Dr.) William E Mayer, who would later become the U.S. Army's chief psychiatrist, revealed that even though there were fewer cases of physical abuse reported in the North Korean POW camps than in prison camps from any other major military conflict throughout history, more men died.

Despite having adequate food, water, and shelter—better physical conditions than POWs in wars before them and after them had—men in the North Korean POW camps experienced the highest POW death rate in American military history. A full 38 percent of the prisoners died. But they didn't die from torture or starvation; they died of extreme hopelessness. Hopelessness that was the result of systematic psychological warfare waged by the North Korean captors.

Mayer's study documented how the North Koreans had employed what he called the "ultimate weapon" of war. Their goal was to deny the men the emotional support that comes from interpersonal relationships.

They devised ways to get the men to inform on each other, promoted self-criticism, found ways to break the prisoners' loyalty to their country and each other, and even went so far as to make sure the men received only negative mail, withholding any supportive correspondence but promptly delivering past due bills and Dear John letters.

With nothing and no one to live for, the men lost their belief in themselves and each other, and they gave up. It was not uncommon for a soldier to go into the corner of his hut alone, put a blanket over his head, and be dead within two days

The soldiers actually referred to it as "give up-itis." Mayer's study revealed that fully half of the prisoners died from it, with no other medical justification for their deaths.

Moved by the story of how negativity literally killed people, Donald Clifton decided to investigate the flip side of the equation. He embarked on a lifelong study of positivity, and over the course of his five-decade career his pioneering work improved the lives of millions. In 2002, he was recognized by the American Psychological Association as not only the Grandfather of Positive Psychology, but also the Father of Strengths Psychology.

Clifton's grandson Tom Rath writes movingly about Don's response to the Korean War POW case in the introduction to *How Full Is Your Bucket*, the bestselling book they coauthored in 2003, completed just weeks before Don succumbed to cancer. Rath says that Don's review of that one specific case study altered the entire focus of his career and his life. Up until that point the field of psychology was based almost entirely on *what is wrong* with people. The Korean War POW case inspired Clifton to spend his lifetime studying *what is right* with people.

And it demonstrates how when we lose love, we've lost everything.

The Triangle of Truth enables you to tap into what is already right with people, and to what is right within yourself. It opens up a space for you to see the good in people and situations, even when the surface information looks bad.

The two POW stories, Stockdale's and the Korean War victims', both of which inspired major bodies of work, reveal much about the power of human emotions. They demonstrate beyond a shadow of a doubt that how we feel affects everything that we do, and our perceptions of every situation we encounter.

These two dramatic scenarios show us the value of human connection, the power of human thought, and why sometimes our very survival depends on our ability to rise above an either/or mind-set.

Why Faith Is Different from Optimism

Stockdale's caution against optimism, saying that the men who thought they were going to get out by Christmas and then didn't were the ones who died of a broken heart, seems to fly in the face of what much of us have always believed about success.

I've always considered myself a sunny-side upper; in fact I think I was probably born an optimist. So when I first heard this advice, it was hard for me to understand why a person wouldn't want to be optimistic. But analyzing the two POW scenarios reveals the subtle yet distinct difference between optimism and faith.

Optimism is usually tied to conditions, a belief or hope that this will happen or that will happen, but faith is tied to something bigger. It's an overarching belief that everything will work out OK, without being married to having things happen in a specific way or at a specific time.

For some it's faith in God, for others it's a belief in the universal order; it might be faith in family or country, or just a general feeling that the world eventually tilts toward the great good, even though the process often takes longer than we'd like.

Words only have the meaning that we attach to them, but when it comes to faith and optimism, there is a significant difference.

It's important to understand the difference between optimism and faith, in the context of the Triangle of Truth, because as Stockdale wisely points out, when you're overly optimistic you tend to ignore the facts. You often get your heart so set on things happening the way you want them to that you inevitably set yourself up for disappointment.

But if you can set aside your attachments to certain outcomes, and instead draw strength from a deep-rooted faith that everything will ultimately be OK, you'll find yourself better able to accept uncertainty and more able to face the facts of a bad situation.

The men who died in the Hanoi Hilton were the men who clung to false optimism and weren't willing to face the facts. Men who died in the Korean POW camps were those who succumbed to pessimism and despair because they had lost their faith in each other, and in the future.

But we don't have to choose between either of these two options. Few of us will ever have to face conditions as horrific as these men did, yet we can learn from these extreme examples.

Just as we descend into either/or thinking when we're dealing with frustrating people, so too do we descend into either/or thinking when we're dealing with frustrating situations.

When we're afraid, or stressed or angry, we often lose our ability to assimilate the brutal facts of the present with faith in the long-term because our minds go to the place where we feel most comfortable. For some that may be optimism, and for others pessimism

When faced with a bad situation, we either ignore the facts, or we focus solely on the negative elements of the problem, losing all hope that the situation will ever get better. Stress and fear cause us to revert to our default settings. Yet neither of these mind-sets serves us.

However, if we can retrain our brains, to pause and make a conscious decision to choose love over fear, we can rise above this pattern. Because when we choose love, we calm ourselves. And when we're calm, we can harness the faith in our hearts, while at the same time summoning the courage to face the facts with a clear-thinking mind.

Assimilating facts and faith is how we make better decisions, and it's a lesson I certainly wish I had learned earlier in my life.

A Very Expensive Lesson

In fall of 2006 my husband and I began the process of purchasing a midsized sign manufacturing company. We closed the deal on January 1, 2007, at the precise moment when the economy had peaked and was about to head down. But we didn't know that at the time.

We bought the company after my husband, a former Fortune 100 executive, left a twenty-three-year corporate career. The company we purchased was a blue-collar business, with seventeen employees who manufactured, sold, and installed big light-up signs (the kind you'd see outside a Wendy's or Gap, both of whom were occasional customers).

Within months it became apparent that the revenues couldn't support the level of debt and that we had overpaid for the company. However, we had invested most of our money into the business, so failure was not an option, or at least not one we were willing to consider—yet.

So we decided that we were going to reorganize, cut costs, and grow sales in order to achieve profitability. Yes, it was going to be tough, but he was a finance and operations guy, and I was a sales and leadership expert, so certainly between the two of us we could turn around a failing midsize sign company. In a better economy our plan might have worked.

As we began the process of making changes, the economy was descending into a free fall. Commercial construction was our bread and butter, and with over 75 percent of our business in putting up new retail signs, we were fairly dependent on retail growth. But during 2007 and 2008, the time period when we were

attempting to turn things around, new commercial construction was coming to a screeching halt.

Competitors began going out of business, and those who were
left were so desperate to get business that they were cutting
prices to the bone, forcing us to reduce our own margins, and at
times even taking losses on jobs just so that we could keep our
people working.

It got to a point where it was a good week if we didn't have
to dip into our credit line or personal savings in order to make
payroll.

As the weeks turned into months, we lost more and more
money, and the stress continued to mount. Every day it was
something worse, and as with most couples experiencing financial problems, it did not bring out the best in either of us.

We alternated between despair and what I now recognize
as delusional optimism. We'd get a major order for a big commercial sign, and everyone would get excited, telling each other
that this was the start of something big. Then the pizza chain or
burger franchise would put a halt to their expansion plans, or
would cut their budget in half, and we'd be right back where we
started with no new work in the pipeline, a mountain of debt,
and a substantial weekly payroll.

It was during this time that I began to fully understand just
how dangerous optimism and pessimism can be to an organization, and sometimes even to a marriage.

In hindsight, I now can see that we were overly optimistic
when we purchased the company, allowing ourselves to believe
the growth picture painted by the former owner. Although we
both know how to read a profit and loss statement and had

pored over the financials, we had allowed enthusiasm to color our analysis.

The plan was that we would buy the company, he would run it, and then after a few years we would sell it and reap huge rewards. It sure sounded good when we said it.

But after the deal was all signed, and we began losing money left and right, it was obvious that our big plan had gone awry.

At first we fell victim to what my husband now refers to as the Christmas mentality. Telling ourselves that things will turn around in the spring, it's just a slow time. When the orders failed to materialize, we'd tell ourselves everyone will want their signs up in time for the holidays. We became just like the prisoners who thought they would get out by Christmas and then became brokenhearted when things didn't turn out like they planned.

When our optimism proved inaccurate we would sink into pessimism, wallowing in self-pity and despair. How could we have been so stupid? Why didn't we spot the problems before we bought the company? Why couldn't we turn things around?

As we alternated between hoping things would get better and fearing that we had made the worst mistake of our lives, we continued to watch the debt mount, and our savings drain.

To make matters even worse, I was a business consultant and my husband was a twenty-five-year finance and ops guy, and while we had certainly experienced setbacks, neither of us had ever failed on this level before. So in addition to the private angst, we also felt that we were facing public embarrassment as well.

Being embarrassed over a business failure during the worst economy since the Depression seems silly now. But the human ego is a powerful thing, and when you're knee-deep in a problem, sometimes it feels like you're the only one this has ever happened to.

Honesty also compels me to admit that I was not the nicest wife during this time. I would love to tell you that I jumped in and helped my husband out, offering kind, wise support whenever he needed it.

But I didn't.

Instead, when the problems were first revealed, I ignored it. I was on a book tour during much of the first few months we owned the company. So unfortunately, when my husband began telling me about the lack of orders and equipment that kept breaking down, I was so focused on my own work that I didn't pay enough attention. I figured, he's a smart guy, he'll solve these problems.

But as it became evident that the problems weren't so easily solvable, and we were in danger of losing most of our money, I jumped in and began shouting directions left and right, second-guessing much of what he had done, giving him big long lists of everything he should be doing differently from this point forward. You can just imagine how loved and supported he felt.

I was giving him much of the advice I would give a client, but instead of serving it up in a nice report, with timelines and a plan, I practically beat him about the head with it every time we sat down to talk. Oh, and did I mention that I frequently brought it up during dinner or on the weekends when the poor man was trying to recharge?

It's funny how when you're under stress everything you know about human nature just flies out the window, because all you can think about is your own survival.

Of course I can now see that the reason I was so frantic was because my overly optimistic nature had been proven wrong, and I, too, was descending into doom and gloom pessimism. But rather than going into the corner of my hut and pulling a blanket over my head, I chose to take it out on everyone else.

What can I say? Sometimes I'm an expert and sometimes I'm just Exhibit A of the problem.

However, order barking aside, eventually it became obvious that all the strategic planning and hard work in the world couldn't overcome a bad economy and too much debt.

The turning point came when my uncle asked us, "Do you see any way you can make any serious money on this business in the next five years?" Our immediate answer was, "No, not really." To which he responded with, "Then why the hell do you keep doing it?"

We had to be willing to let go of our fear of failure in order to start making better decisions. So we made a conscious decision to choose love. Up until that point we had allowed fear to dominate our thinking; but when we made the decision to choose love, we became calmer and, quite frankly, smarter.

We decided that our love for each other and our love for our kids called on us to be more disciplined in our thinking. We needed to look clear-eyed at the facts and make decisions, not based on what we hoped might happen in the future, but on where we actually were today. We also decided that our marriage and our family were bigger than a business failure. On the scale of human suffering we were still some of the lucky ones. People had certainly survived worse problems, so we would survive this.

We decided that this experience was going to be part of the

larger story of our lives, and that we would learn from it and find a way to turn it to the greater good, even if we weren't sure what that would look like. That faith enabled us to face the hard facts of a bad situation.

It would be nice if I could tell you that things turned around, and that we made a boatload of money. But they didn't. We ultimately decided to close the company, turning it back over to the former owner, walking away with a big pile of debt and a good part of our savings gone.

But we did learn something. Things are sometimes clearer in the rearview mirror, and I now see where vacillating between optimism and pessimism caused us problems on every level. Optimism prompted us to get in too quickly and prevented us from facing the ugly facts for far too long. Then when things got so bad that we couldn't gloss over it anymore, pessimism caused us to bicker and fight, dividing us, just when we needed each other the most.

Had we been more disciplined about assessing the facts in the beginning we would have never gotten in. Had we had more faith in ourselves and the world's ability to point us in the right direction, we would have gotten out quicker, because we wouldn't have been so afraid to fail.

It was a tough lesson to learn, and it cost us twenty years of good financial planning.

Ironically enough, the day my husband signed the final paperwork was February 13, 2009, the day before Valentine's Day. It was painful, but we decided that the Valentine's Day timing was no accident and that in the arc of our lives it would forever serve as a reminder to us that no matter how bad things get, we can always choose love.

For me, someone who errs on the side of optimism, choosing love is a call for me to pay closer attention to the facts. For others it may be a call to hold on to your faith no matter what. Most of us tend to gravitate toward one side of the facts *And* faith Triangle or the other. But when we choose love, it calls on us to discipline ourselves to embrace both elements.

The postscript on this story is that my husband now works full-time with me in our training and consulting practice, and our business has never been better. We ultimately decided that the world doesn't really need any more big light-up signs, but that people do need help becoming more loving, compassionate, and open-minded. We also realized that coming together to do meaningful work was a better foundation for our lives than simply trying to make a lot of money. Money and meaning are another duality that we're still working to master, but we're getting closer every day.

It wasn't until we let go of our attachment to how we thought things should be that we were able to look clear-eyed at what already was, and to open the door to what could be.

One of the keys to making the Triangle of Truth work is letting go of your attachments to having things a certain way.

When you're stuck in fear, you tend to see situations as either/or. You find yourself thinking, either things go the way I want, or everything is awful. And it doesn't even have be something as dramatic as surviving a POW camp or losing your family business. The fear of not getting our way shows up in all kinds of situations.

I once witnessed a neighborhood meeting where people arguing over what type of fence to install became so angry that they found themselves assaulting each other's characters. The root of all the angst? One group wanted an iron fence and the other group wanted wood. What started out as a nice neighborhood discussion degenerated into a shouting match, as the fear of having to live life looking at a fence chosen by the other guys took over.

Like I said, sometimes fear shows up where we might least expect it.

When you make a conscious decision to choose love, it calms you down, in big situations and small. It gives you the strength to look at the facts, without feeling panicked if things look bad. And loving something bigger than yourself is also what gives you the courage to hold on to faith in the face of adverse conditions.

Two Game-Changing Dualities

Choosing love over fear enables us to assimilate the two most challenging yet fundamental dualities:

- ▸ Everyone is flawed *And* everyone is fabulous,

- ▸ Unflinching assessment of facts *And* unwavering faith.

If you can assimilate these two sets of seemingly competing truths on an intellectual, emotional, and spiritual level, you will literally change the trajectory of your entire life.

Embracing the flawed and fabulous duality of people changes the way you approach them, and facing facts with faith changes the way you approach situations. If you change the way you approach people and the way you approach situations, you've pretty much changed the way you approach life.

Accepting the good and bad in everyone puts you at peace with people, and embracing facts with faith puts you at peace with circumstances.

These are the two most crucial Truth Triangles because they require a change of mind, heart, and spirit.

Life coach and *O Magazine* columnist Martha Beck once wrote, "Just one mental shift switches your psychological setting so that your life automatically improves in many ways you may think are unrelated."

I'm asking you to make two mental shifts, but trust me, it will change pretty much everything. Because when you embrace these two dualities, you're no longer afraid, and suddenly your whole life begins to look and feel different. You no longer have to worry validating someone else's truth will negate your own, or that acknowledging an awful situation means that things will be hopeless forever.

Imagine what might happen if you approached everything grounded in these two thoughts:

1. I don't have all the answers, but I'm willing to see the other side of people.

2. I don't know the end of the story, but I'm willing to face the facts because I have faith that everything will eventually be OK.

How might this affect your relationships? Or your job, or your parenting, your politics, or heck, even your sex life? What might your interactions with others be like if they had this mentality?

Letting go of your attachments isn't about passive acceptance, quite the opposite. It's about meeting the world where it is and seeing people and situations for what they are, because only then will you be able to create something different.

When you try to bend the world to your will, people and circumstances tend to resist. But when we rise above our fears and the human need to control everything, we lift ourselves out of the either/or mind-set that so frequently flatlines our brains.

Being willing to tolerate ambiguity and uncertainty is the only way to open ourselves up to the possibility of *And*.

Embracing *And* means bringing your best intentions and your best ideas into every situation, while at the same time letting go of your attachment to having things play out in certain ways. It means applying every ounce of your intellect to making things better, while also holding a space in your heart for the ideas and emotions of other people.

It means showing up at your best, even when things are at their worst.

The Secret to Mastering the Triangle

The Triangle model enables us to rise above our fears, be they petty or large, and to become smarter than we have been in the past. But we must make a conscious decision to use it.

You can't assimilate the flawed and fabulous nature of people, or combine facts with faith when you're afraid. When we let the lizard take over, our ability to tolerate ambiguity is lost. We lock down on one side or the other and our opportunity to create something better is gone.

But it's not gone forever; it's only gone for a nanosecond. At any given moment in our lives, we are always free to choose love.

The potential for love and fear exists within each of us. Fear is your lesser instincts and it keeps you trapped on the line, forever arguing your position. Love is your higher self, and it's the secret of lifting your heart and soul toward a larger purpose.

We have all kinds of excuses for choosing the path of fear: my life is tough, my in-laws are awful, I'm struggling with money. We complain, we whine, and we offer all kinds of logical reasons to justify a negative belief system.

But at the end of the day, as long as we stay stuck in fear, life will always be an either/or game. Fear keeps us trapped in the limiting beliefs of the human ego. Love enables us to tap into the limitless capacity of the human soul. Love elevates our thinking, but fear just dumbs everything down.

> At the end of the day, as long as we stay stuck in fear, life will always be an either/or game.

I don't know what your future holds, but I do know that good things can come out of bad situations, and that there's probably something wonderful waiting for you on the other side of whatever challenge you may be facing.

If you let it, love can fuel you with the courage to face uncertainty with faith, and it will elevate your mind enough to assimilate what lesser thinkers still believe are contradictory truths.

Either/or thinking is for people who are unable to tolerate uncertainty, and who are too afraid to create anything different than what they've already got.

I'm thinking you're probably smarter than that, though. In fact, I'm sure you are.

Hold Space for Other Perspectives

Solving the Your Agenda Versus My Agenda Quagmire

The highest possible stage in
moral culture is when we recognize that
we ought to control our thoughts.
—CHARLES DARWIN

"At a certain point it gets to be about me, right?"

He was a seasoned salesperson who had been in the business for years, and when he asked me this question near the end of the seminar I was giving, I knew that he was struggling.

It was a legitimate question. After spending the better part of two days practicing how to get inside the mind of the customer, and being constantly reminded by me, "This isn't about you, this is about the customer," the poor fellow was wondering if he was ever going to get to pitch his product.

In his way of thinking, you could either organize your conversation around the customer's world or you could talk about what you were trying to sell. He certainly saw the benefits of asking the customer questions and learning about their goals, to better frame up his point. But as he succinctly pointed out, "You're there to sell them something. At a certain point the call is eventually going to have to be about that."

This was a smart, well-intentioned, nice guy who was trying to do right by his company, his customers, and also his family. However, like many of us, he believed that he had to choose between two agendas. *It's either going to be about me, or it's going to be about you. We might go back and forth during the conversation, but at the end of day, I need to accomplish something and I'm going to make sure I get it done.*

And that's the quagmire.

We often think, in fact we're frequently told, that the most effective way to achieve our objectives is to single-mindedly focus on our goals. A goal orientation itself is not a bad thing. However, problems arise when we become so focused on our own goals that we don't leave space for anyone else's. We become so determined to get our way that we often alienate the very people we are trying to convince.

> **Problems arise when we become so focused on our own goals that we don't leave space for anyone else's.**

How many times have you seen someone so eager to prove their point that nobody else stands a chance? Sometimes even people who agree with them are turned off when it becomes obvious that all they care about is getting their way.

On the flip side, many of us have also experienced the frustration of being so accommodating to others that our *own* agenda is completely forgotten, which only breeds anger and resentment over time.

The Triangle of Truth model provides a way for you to assimilate your agenda with the agenda of someone else, without losing sight of either person's set of objectives. The Triangle model enables you to jettison the either/or thinking that causes us to focus exclusively on ourselves or to forgo our needs in favor of the other guy.

The belief that we have to choose between our agenda and the other guy's is a common problem. It's reinforced by our culture and by political parties that stress beating the opponent more than actually solving the problems. By an educational system that expects teachers to pour mountains of information into their students' heads without providing the time or space for the students to add their own thoughts. And by advertising campaigns that spin out sexy thirty-second pitches, encouraging us to buy something today before we have time to think about whether or not we really want or need it.

Is it any surprise that the well-intended salesman is wondering when it's going to be about him? Everywhere he turns he hears a one-way pitch from someone else. He might have spent two days in my seminar being taught how to ask questions and listen, but I guarantee you the majority of communication from his company is all about making quota and how great their products are.

The idea that we have to choose between our agenda and someone else's is reinforced at multiple levels, and it's also the default setting of our own minds. But people who can rise above this tendency and think bigger than just their own agenda actually have more success accomplishing their goals.

Compare the "when is it going to be about me?" salesman with another salesperson I once worked with.

The Sales Rep Who Loved

Air-conditioning may have improved life in the South, but even a two-minute walk from the air-conditioned car to the air-conditioned doctor's office had me dripping with sweat.

My blouse was stuck to my back before 10 a.m., but I was working with one of the best sales reps I'd ever seen, and I was willing to suffer the sweltering South Texas heat just to watch her work.

Her name was Karen, and it was obvious from the first call that she was a superstar. Smart as a whip, she remembered everything about everyone.

She sold pharmaceuticals, calling on doctors, nurses, and hospitals, and wherever she went, people's faces lit up the moment she walked in the door. Doctors even asked her for her opinion. To put this into perspective, most of the time it's hard for a rep to even see a doctor, much less get one to talk. In many cases, salespeople wind up practically chasing doctors down the hall trying to get their attention with some new piece of research data. But the doctors stopped to speak with Karen and actually had a two-way conversation. If case you're wondering, yes, she was attractive. But not any more so than most of the other reps in her industry, and she got the exact same reaction from men and women, no matter what their age. In several instances, elderly patients made a point of coming up to her to say hello.

It was almost like people were under a spell. In one instance an office manager was on the phone, clearly arguing with an insurance company, yet when she saw Karen, she told the person on the other end of the line, "I have to go, my rep is here." Who knows how long this overworked, overwhelmed office manager had been on hold waiting to speak to a live body at the insurance company, but in walks Karen, and even though she's clearly in the middle of a conversation, she puts down the phone and basically clears the deck so she can talk to a sales rep! If you've ever been in sales, especially medical sales, you know that this almost never happens.

After several hours of watching Karen elicit similar responses from other customers, I, too, was under her spell. As she drove me back to the airport, I knew that I had to find out just what made her tick. So with thirty minutes left before I had to catch my flight, I decided to see if I could get inside the head of a superstar.

I'll never forget the story she told me. When I asked her about how her year was going, she told me that she was the number one rep in the country. She said that being number one had been her goal from the day she started. She had plotted out exactly what it would take to get to the top and within her first year, she achieved it. Big surprise, a super-successful person with measurable time-bound goals, go figure.

But when I asked her, "What do you think about before you go on calls?" her answer was anything but standard corporate fare.

"Well," she said, "it's kind of weird and I don't tell many people this, but have you ever seen that movie *What the BLEEP Do We Know!*?"

I had seen the movie, in fact I saw it multiple times, and had even purchased it on DVD for my family. It was kind of a documentary meets drama meets animation hybrid of a movie that served up a blend of quantum physics and spirituality. It wound up being very successful, but at the time of our conversation, not many people had seen it beyond the spiritual seeker crowd, and certainly not many in the corporate world. So I was a bit surprised that she had not only seen it, but was referencing it.

One of the major premises of the movie is that our thoughts create our reality, on both a physical and a spiritual level, and this is what she began to talk about.

"You know how one of the scientists in the movie said, you can create your day by just envisioning it each morning?" she asked.

"Yes, I remember that part very well."

"My husband and I liked that idea, so we started to do it. Every morning we lie in bed, and we make sure we're holding hands or lying right next to each other, and then we create our days. We talk about what we want to happen and how things will unfold. I envision people responding positively to me, smiling when I walk in the door, doctors asking me questions, patients feeling better."

"That's it?" I said. "These people are under a spell because you and your husband imagined it while you were lying in the bed?"

Here I am in one of the most buttoned-up corporate environments in America, and the number one sales rep is telling me she owes her success to the advice of a woo-woo movie?

"Well, there is one other thing," she said. "I also always make a point to think about the patients, one in particular."

She went on to describe how her product, a drug used to treat a variety of debilitating conditions, improved people's lives. She shared several touching stories about the impact it had on individual patients, and as she told me about one woman who, because her symptoms had been lessened, was now able to spend time with her grandkids, her eyes filled with tears. "I'll never forget her," she said. "She came up to me when I was talking with one of my doctors and told me how her whole life had been changed. I think about her every single day. Whenever I'm talking to a difficult doctor, or dealing with a frustrated nurse, or an uncooperative insurance company, my mind always goes back to that one grandmother. My mission is to help her and people just like her, and I know that everyone I deal with wants to help her just as much as I do."

Here Karen was earning big bonuses and winning incentive trips, yet when asked about her sales success, she was moved to tears talking about the patients she helps.

And therein lies the difference.

Is it any wonder that people respond so positively to Karen? Good grief, she shows up for work every day holding a vision of helping an aging grandmother in her heart. Compare that to a salesperson who is constantly worried about making his quota and wondering when it's going to be his turn to talk.

Who do you think gives off a better vibe?

Like it or not, the thoughts going through your head affect the way other people respond to you. Frequently the vibe you give off at the beginning of an interaction is what determines the outcome you wind up with at the end.

Why Your Body Is Smarter
Than Your Brain

We all know that our mood affects our body language, and we also instinctively recognize when someone else is thinking negative thoughts.

Dr. Richard Strozzi-Heckler, founder of the Strozzi Institute, has spent his lifetime studying the mind, body, spirit interface, and he uses Somatics—the unity of language, action, feeling, and meaning—to teach executives how to better align their bodies with their messages.

Strozzi-Heckler says, "When people listen only 7% is content, the other 93% is body presence, which includes your tone of voice." That's why when someone gives off a negative vibe, it doesn't really matter what they say—the message of their body is what you'll take away.

Through the work of Strozzi-Heckler and others, we are beginning to more fully understand just how powerfully our thoughts affect our daily interactions, and the way that others respond to us. Now thanks to neuroscience, machines can actually see how different places in our brains are activated when we're thinking different thoughts.

Strozzi-Heckler has found that when you are in a zone of deep authenticity and deep care, a certain part of your brain is activated. Your thoughts then radiate out through your body, sending a clear message to anyone you interact with.

However, if the fear and angst part of your brain has been activated, people will feel less comfortable with you, and they won't be as attracted to you, even if they don't know why.

Strozzi-Heckler says, "The human mind is always scanning for trust and credibility." That means people are constantly subconsciously reading each other. And when they read angst, or aggression, they either turn away or respond in kind.

Your thoughts affect how you hold your body, your facial expression, and also the tone of voice you use, all of which convey a loud and clear message.

When someone like Karen shows up, thinking about the grandmother she wants to help, she radiates out those caring thoughts at every level of her being, and that in turn creates a positive response in just about everyone she meets. Contrast that with someone thinking, "When is it going to be about me?" and it's easy to see why Karen is at the top of the heap.

Once again, it's the difference between showing up with love in your heart and being afraid that you might not get your way.

What do you think your body is broadcasting if you approach an interaction or potential conflicts thinking, this is never going to work, or I'm going to have to be really aggressive in order to get my way, or worse, this other person is sooo wrong, and I'm going to prove it?

However, what might happen if you went into those same situations holding on to the faith that you will ultimately find a solution that works for everyone? And believing that the people on the other side want the best outcome just as much as you do?

It goes beyond just wanting to be helpful; it's about showing up with a sincere desire to directly connect with other people. People can feel the difference when someone truly cares about their side of the Triangle.

Which was another underpinning of Karen's success. Yes, she wanted to be number one, but when she went on calls she wasn't thinking about her quota or how she might make the sale. She thought about the grandmother, and she also held a vision of people responding positively to her. Not of her convincing them, but of them responding in an authentically positive way.

The nuance is important, because many of her peers and competitors may be envisioning the grand moment when a customer agrees to their plan and helps get them one step closer to making a big bonus. Karen is thinking about it from the customer's perspective. Envisioning the look on their faces, and how they might be feeling and acting during the interaction. And she also looks behind their busyness and frustrations to discern their good intent.

The reason Karen consistently gets a better response than her peers, as evidenced by her number one status, is because she and other top performers like her are literally coming from a different place in their brains.

What the World of Sales
Teaches Us About Assimilating Truths

Over the course of my twenty-five-year career, I've observed thousands of sales calls, everything from people selling two-dollar widgets to huge presentations for multimillion-dollar consulting projects. I've spent countless hours hovering in the back of conference rooms, standing in the middle of hospital hallways, and sometimes even sweltering in the heat of parking lots watching salespeople give their pitches.

It might not sound exciting to the average person, but for me, it's been an observational gold mine. I've had the opportunity to study and document the human condition up close and personal. For over two decades, much of my life's work has been devoted to understanding how the behavior of one person affects the behavior of another.

I've served as leadership coach and consultant, helping managers identify and communicate strategy, and as a speech writer and coach, helping executives craft their messages so that audiences will respond in the way that they want them to.

All of them are different forms of selling, and over the years I've seen everything from the awful to the amazing. I've ridden alongside sales reps who bombed every call, seemingly oblivious to the fact that their customers couldn't wait for them to leave. I've also witnessed presentations where people walked in ready to tell the presenter why he or she was wrong; yet thirty minutes later the audience was eagerly supporting everything that the presenter said, simply because of the way the information and ideas were served up.

And by studying both the fabulous and the not so fabulous, I've been able to discern why some people consistently get others to go along with their plans while other people are left wondering why things never seem to go their way.

Some people may be turned off by the idea of sales, assuming that it's about manipulating people, or getting them to do something that they really don't want to do. But it's only bad salespeople who do that, the kind whose companies encourage them to use calculated, manipulative scripts, or who just want to close a single transaction and never see you again.

Superstars like Karen are anything but self-serving. I've had the opportunity to work with hundreds of truly fabulous salespeople who wake up every single day determined to do their best for their customers, and who bring energy, enthusiasm, and passion into everything they do. Those are the people we can emulate.

It doesn't matter whether you're trying to convince your spouse to take out the trash more often, your team to get on board with a new initiative, or your neighbor to agree to your choice of fence. When you're trying to get someone else to go along with your line of thinking, you're selling. Yes, I know they should probably be doing it anyway, and you shouldn't have to convince them. But they're not, so it's up to you to help them see the light.

> **When you're trying to get someone else to go along with your line of thinking, you're selling.**

The Triangle of Truth is a tool for assimilating your agenda with the agenda of someone else. By analyzing the techniques of the superstar salespeople, we gain valuable information that can be applied to our own challenges and conflicts.

Salespeople are charged with selling a product or service, yet if they don't pay attention to their customer's agenda they won't be successful. It's a classic my agenda *And* your agenda situation.

Yet I can tell you that there's a distinct difference between average salespeople and those who are truly stellar at their jobs.

The people who consistently get others to buy into their agendas have a totally different thought process than their less successful counterparts. So by crawling inside the brains of super successful salespeople, we can learn the secret of getting our own interactions to go the way we want them to.

What Differentiates the Superstars

Organizations are always trying to figure out what differentiates the best salespeople from the mediocre ones. Is it better questions, more thorough planning, a better understanding of the customers, more sales activity? Everyone is looking for the magic bullet.

Why are some people able to get everyone to do what they want, while other people in the same situation, selling the same stuff, have a much lower rate of success? People have been trying to crack the code on sales success ever since the first hay salesman hit the road with his pushcart. It's also a leadership challenge: why do some leaders get buy in, while others struggle to get the team on board?

The difference between good and bad performance is usually fairly obvious. The truly poor performers are the people who can't show up on time, who are consistently unprepared, and who don't take their job very seriously. But the difference between the average performers and the superstars is much more subtle and harder to quantify. However, I've studied this across a variety of industries—read "5 Secrets of Sales Superstars" on www .TriangleofTruth.com—and while the nuances vary, the difference between the people who are merely good at influencing others versus the people who are truly great at it always comes back to a fundamental difference in thoughts.

Average performers tend to be focused on their goals. They understand their product or service offering, and they can usually tell you where they stand in the company rankings on any given day.

The superstars have a different agenda. Spend any time with any superstar performer and you'll discover that in addition to wanting to be successful within their own organizations, they're also equally passionate about their customer's goals. And they don't just act like they care about their customers, they actually do.

They're like Karen. They know their side of the Triangle, but they also care just as deeply about the person on the other side. That fundamental difference plays out in their every interaction. That's why they ask better questions, do more thorough planning, and have more extensive customer files. It's not just that they're more skilled, it's that they have an entirely different internal motivation.

Average salespeople can usually do a pretty good job of talking about their product and service in a compelling way. But superstars are able to seamlessly assimilate their agendas with their customers' agendas because instead of just thinking about their own information, they're also always proactively thinking about their customers as well.

It makes sense; the people who better connect with their customers sell more stuff. I'm sure you've seen this same dynamic play out in sales and customer service interactions that you were involved in, be it buying a house, a car, or even a new cell phone plan.

People who focus solely on their own agenda aren't as successful as the people who take the time to figure out what's going on with the other person. It's a lesson we all know, but one we frequently forget.

But the difference between the results you get when you're thinking about yourself and the results you get when you're also thinking about the other person is sometimes so dramatically divergent that it almost seems to defy logic.

Same Message, Different Results

One of the industries I've spent a lot of time in is the pharmaceutical business, and for a variety of reasons, pharmaceutical sales calls are the perfect case study for understanding how a person's thoughts can affect the outcome of an interaction.

The pharma world is extremely regulated. There are strict rules about what salespeople can and cannot say. You can't tell a doctor that your drug cures cancer if it doesn't. Everything has to go through legal, including all the sales and marketing materials.

So when a rep calls on a doctor or other health care professional trying to sell them on the benefits of their drug, they have to stick to the preapproved messages. Which means that all the reps from any given company are all saying virtually the same thing on their calls.

But here's where it gets interesting. Time and time again, I've watched two reps present the exact same information, yet get completely different responses.

One rep will make twenty calls showing doctors his or her latest drug data, and get about a 30 or 40 percent positive response rate. A large percentage of the customers will be unwilling to even listen and many who do listen are clearly just waiting for the rep to finish so that they can get back to their work.

Another rep in the same company will take that exact same information and make twenty calls on the same type of customers, sometimes even in the same city, and get an 80 or even 90 percent positive response rate. Customers who would have typically disconnected had a mediocre rep presented the information will find that same information practically riveting when it's presented by a superstar.

It's a dynamic I've seen play out time and time again, across numerous organizations, and it has nothing to do with age or gender. I've witnessed doctors in the same hospital ignore data when it's presented by one salesperson, but tell another salesperson that the exact same data was interesting and they'd like to see more. It almost defies logic. Especially when you consider that in this case, the customers are scientists and medical professionals who are trained to look primarily at facts. Yet what causes the biggest difference in responses has nothing to do with the scientific data at all; the only difference is the interpersonal skills of the person delivering it.

Top-performing salespeople present the exact same information, using the exact same words and the exact same materials, as their more mediocre counterparts, yet they get a completely different response.

Why?

Because the best salespeople aren't afraid. They have faith that things will work out, so they apply every bit of their energy toward connecting with the other person. It's not about them, it's about the other person.

Customer loyalty expert Chip Bell likens the difference

between people who focus on themselves and people who focus on the customer to the difference in two performances of, ironically enough, *Death of a Salesman.*

Bell says, "When I was in high school I saw *Death of a Salesman* and it was pretty good. Yet years later I saw Dustin Hoffman perform it, and even though it was the exact same script, it was a totally different experience." What was the difference? One group of actors was worried about memorizing their lines and whether or not their girlfriend was watching from the second row. But Dustin Hoffman was focused on creating an experience for the audience.

Like a nervous actor, mediocre salespeople are often secretly afraid that they'll fail or that they won't make their quota and get to go on the year-end bonus trip, so they can't connect as authentically with the person standing in front of them.

Fear, even when it's subtle, creates a barrier between them and the people they're trying to convince. They don't have the seamless mind, body, spirit alignment that the Karens of the world do, and their customers can feel the difference.

Keep in mind, most salespeople in the pharmaceutical world are smart, hardworking, polished professionals. Big drug companies depend on them to represent them in the medical community, so they're not going to send out a bunch of sloppy slackers. Pharmaceutical sales jobs pay well, so companies can afford to be choosy. The interview process is quite extensive and the people are always well trained.

So why are the differences so stark? Why does one group of well-trained professionals show up confident that they will be able to assimilate both sides of the Triangle, while the other group is frequently only thinking about their side of things?

The difference lies in the way that the two groups define success.

A Subtle Shift of Focus

Karen's misty-eyed comment about waking up every day thinking about helping people like the aging grandmother illustrates one of the key factors that separate people who achieve greatness from those who stay stuck in mediocrity.

Average performers are focused on their own goals; but superstars, people like Karen, are motivated by something bigger than themselves and it drives their every thought and action.

They don't hold a vision of their comp plan in their hearts. They hold a vision of how people's lives might be better, and you can feel it with every word they speak.

Superstars go for the top of the Triangle. To them, success isn't just about achieving their goals, it's about coming together with other people to achieve something much more meaningful. And that larger vision of success makes all the difference in the world.

Top performers know that they don't have to choose between making money and making a difference. They do both. And it's not just because Karen happens to sell life-changing medication. Across all the industries I've worked in, holding a vision of something larger than themselves is the common denominator behind all the great performers.

▸ The top-performing Apple Computer rep who practically beams when he talks about how exciting it is to help people streamline their businesses, and harness their creativity.

▶ The medical equipment rep who told me that her father had been a doctor who worked long hours, and because of that she always wanted to make other doctors' lives easier.

▶ The Tupperware distributor who told me how she changed people's lives with plastic bowls by giving women a chance to be successful on their own terms.

When asked about their jobs, each and every one of them talks about the impact that they have on others, and they get emotional during the conversation. While their counterparts may be able to rattle off a list of generic reasons why their products or services are so great, the superstars hold a clear vision of the way they impact other people's lives.

And it isn't just super-successful salespeople and entrepreneurs who think this way. Top performers in every field almost always have a similar make-life-better-for-others orientation. For example:

▶ One of my favorite CEO clients says, "I'm not really creating a company. I'm creating a community of people who care."

▶ A franchise owner whose company provides services for the elderly says, "I help improve people's relationship with their parents, and I provide seniors with the dignity and respect they deserve."

▶ A top-performing teacher talks about how she struggled as a student and says it's her mission to help the kids whose brains work differently.

▶ Great parents are always conscious of the fact that they are raising future world leaders.

While their average-performing colleagues and counterparts are just going through the motions, or thinking about how they can gain market share, or get promotions, or get through the day, or win the big incentive trip to Aruba, top performers have their eyes on a totally different prize.

Other people aren't obstacles, or even potential helpers, in accomplishing their goals. Other people *are* their goal. They can see both the forest and the trees. They connect their daily actions to the big picture because they're thinking about both sides of the Triangle as well as the top.

One might argue that most of us want to make life better for others. After all, who goes into teaching or becomes a parent or runs a department with the goal of making people unhappy?

But the difference isn't who wants the best versus who wants the worst. It's much more subtle. It's the difference between an attachment to our own personal agenda and a vision of success that's large enough for others.

How You Organize Your Mind

Average performers tend to go into interactions determined to show their clients exactly how they can help, or demonstrate to their colleagues why their ideas are the best, or explain to their spouse why their plan is the most logical solution, and that agenda dominates their thinking.

While superstars may know how their ideas or services can

improve peoples' lives, their thoughts and actions are directed at connecting with each individual person so that they can figure out how they can be the most helpful in each unique situation.

Going back to Karen, her company had plenty of competition, and in many situations the doctors and other providers preferred the competing drugs. However, although Karen knew her competitive advantages, unlike her single-minded counterparts, the "why our stuff is better and why you should do what I suggest" mantra wasn't her primary thought track. She talked about her products' advantages when appropriate, but the overarching theme of her work, the refrain that was constantly playing in her head, was to help people—to help the patients, to help the doctors, to help the nurses, and even to help the insurance companies.

Average-performing people tend to view others as potential helpers or hindrances in accomplishing their agendas. If someone says something that feels out of alignment with their goals, they're quick to tell them why that's not correct, and even though it may look like they're listening, their bodies convey the message that they don't like what the other person is saying.

Superstars think of other people as partners, and it's not just some lame line they heard in a training program, or something their company touts in the annual report. For true superstars, partnering with people is a way of life. So when someone else shares information, even if it feels contradictory to their agenda, they are sincerely interested in what the other person has to say.

The reason superstar salespeople are able to assimilate their company's agenda with their customers' agendas is their minds aren't stuck in either/or. They know they don't have to decide between their needs and their customers' needs. They hold a space for the other person's agenda, and make it their mission to understand where the other person is coming from because they're going for the top of the Triangle. They truly want a solution that's great for everyone, so they listen better, ask more questions, and every fiber of their body conveys, "I actually care about what you think."

The difference between superstar and mediocre sales reps is a business example, but the "my agenda versus your agenda" quagmire plays out in almost every area of life.

- ► How many times do we pay lip service to the idea of collaborating when we really just want things to go our way?

- ► How often do we try to get our colleagues to support our ideas without even considering how they might be impacted?

- ► How many times do we act like we're listening, when we really just want the other person to quit talking so we can share our knowledge?

- ► How often do we strategize about the best way to get someone to agree with us, without ever considering he or she may have different and perhaps even better ideas?

- ► How frequently do we think about our spouse as the person who is supposed to help us with our plans versus someone who might have plans of their own?

Allowing your own agenda to dominate your thinking prevents you from using the Triangle of Truth because it creates a barrier between you and others. People can feel it when you're only focused on your own goals, and they instinctively react defensively.

Sex and relationship expert Michael Alvear, who spent three seasons as the host of the UK and HBO hit show *The Sex Inspectors*, describes how the my agenda versus your agenda battle often surfaces in intimate relationships:

> *The most common problem we encountered on the show was the frustration men had about the infrequency of sex with their wives or girlfriends, who were exhausted from work/housework/raising children. It always baffled me as to why such an easy problem couldn't be solved (we literally had a mantra for men: "If you want more sex, do more housework.")*
>
> *Even when the men could see their women were tired, even when women broadcast it to them, it didn't seem to matter. It took so little to get so much, yet the men wouldn't do it. The race to prove who's hurt more (the woman who feels burdened by the man or the man who feels rejected by the woman) blinded both parties to what really mattered—the expression of their love. Their inability to see what mattered to their partner robbed them from the very thing they wanted. It literally came down to a man saying, "I'd rather not do the dishes than to have sex with the woman I love." Truly, it was that absurd...*

It's worth noting that the women were just as stubborn in not giving their partners what *they* were asking for. In the race to prove who's hurt, both parties lost.

It can be challenging to let go of an attachment to your own agenda, but when the stakes are high, sometimes it pays to be the person who is willing to do it first.

It's Not You, It's Me
(So Please Stick to the Subject)

But why is it difficult? Why do some people continue to cling to the belief that they have to choose between agendas, while the superstars of work and life instinctively understand that you don't?

It all goes back to being willing to tolerate uncertainty.

Top performers, in every field—be it relationships, business, politics—have enough confidence in their solution to put it aside for a while, and turn their laserlike focus toward better understanding the person standing in front of them. They're confident that they will ultimately be able to help, but they aren't attached to having it play out in a certain way.

That combination, a high confidence level that you can help but with no attachment to a particular path, coupled with a very sincere desire to do your best for others, is the secret of being able to tolerate the potential ambiguity of putting your own goals on hold.

Top performers, be they salespeople, executives, parents, or community volunteers, know their side of the Triangle; they know it cold. Every top performer I've ever worked with has always had an extremely wide and deep knowledge in their area of expertise, but rather than using that information as the organizing basis for their interactions, they make it their mission to get inside the other person's head first.

Much like the open-minded in-law who doesn't allow one truth about someone to define their entire perception, superstars file their agenda in one place, and then direct their energy toward adding to that information.

Average performers often spend their time trying to prove the accuracy of their own information. Superstars spend their time trying to uncover the other person's truths so that they can build something together.

People who are the most successful at influencing others are those who are willing to put their side of the Triangle on pause. Not forever, but long enough to spend much of their face-to-face interactions trying to understand the other person's perspective.

They ask questions before they start talking about themselves, and they listen to the answers, knowing full well that the information the other person reveals may require them to change their approach.

They can tolerate the uncertainty because they're confident that at some point a path will be revealed and they'll see a way to build on both their agendas and get to the top.

But I want to be very clear on a specific nuance, particularly when it comes to sales. Superstars don't just go in and say, "I'm here to serve, so how can I help you?" That's certainly their mental orientation, but they don't go about it willy-nilly or expect the customer to figure things out where they—the salesperson—can be of the most use.

Superstars are extremely disciplined about applying every bit of their brains and talent toward figuring out exactly what is going on with the other person so that they can come up with suggestions for helping them. They're the one who wants to make the sale, so they understand that it's not the customers' job to figure out where they might be useful—it's theirs.

They work long and hard, both mentally and physically, to put themselves in the other person's shoes. Every fiber of their being says, I'm smart, I've done my homework, I have some ideas about how I might help you, but the most important thing to me right now is what's going on with you.

You might be thinking at this point, well, duh, salespeople are supposed to figure out how to help their customers, What does that have to do with helping me deal with my crazy narrow-minded neighbor or getting my budget passed at work or helping me show the other committee chairs at church why they shouldn't get all the money? It's not like I'm going to walk in and say please tell me what your needs are and then I'll cave and give you everything you want.

You might not want to phrase it that way, but an ability to put your own agenda on pause, even momentarily, and find out where the other person is coming from, is the basis for all successful interactions.

The people who go into a situation determined to get their way give off an oppositional energy. People who go in trying to serve the greater good inevitably get a better response.

Most of us believe that we approach situations trying to achieve the greater good. Politicians believe that their party has the best way to solve problems, bickering couples each believe that they want a happy marriage, and average-performing salespeople usually believe that their products are truly helpful.

But here's the difference. It isn't about who wants to do the right thing versus who doesn't. It's who is firmly attached to their own agenda versus who is open to co-creating the best possible solution for everyone.

Once More with Feeling

We often assume that our circumstances cause our emotions, but that's not true at all. Our thoughts cause emotions. It's not a good or bad thing happening to you that causes you to be happy or upset. It's the thoughts you attach to it.

For example, the power goes out and leaves you and your family in the dark for six hours. You can either think, "Oh no, all the food in my freezer might go bad," or you can think, "Wow, six hours to sit by the fire with my family." Your emotions will follow your thoughts accordingly.

Buddha said, "We are formed and molded by our thoughts. Those whose minds are shaped by selfless thoughts give joy when they speak or act. Joy follows them like a shadow that never leaves them."

Information sounds different when it comes from people who hold a vision of a larger purpose, because they're thinking different thoughts when they deliver it. Their mind-set isn't, "Oh, I hope I get my agenda through." Instead, they think, "I hope we can create something great for everyone." These higher-level thoughts create the powerful positive emotions that other people instinctively respond to.

I know that the popular book and movie *The Secret* tells us that envisioning riches can bring you a new house or car. I'm all for visualizing success, and if you can get yourself a new BMW by simply imagining it, more power to you. However, I suspect that the Universe is probably more responsive to a drug sales-person's desire to help heal the sick than it is to someone who just wants to make their bonus so they can buy a new Rolex.

A Question of Timing

Go back to the sales example. While all the salespeople present the exact same information, what differentiates the superstars is not just how they say it, but when.

Most salespeople know they're supposed to ask the customer questions before they start talking about their product or service. And most organizations usually teach their people a sales call model that includes questions at the start of the interaction.

The difference between mediocre people and the superstars is often the intent of their questions.

Mediocre salespeople show up ready to share, so their questions are always obviously trying to tee up an opportunity for them to deliver their pitch. They ask things like, "If I could show you a way to help address this condition, would you be interested?" or "Don't you think XYZ is a big problem?"

Which is really just a semipolite way of saying, "I'm trying to get you to say something that will give me permission to talk."

The superstars show up to ready to learn and connect so their questions have more depth and are designed to help them truly understand the person on the other side of the Triangle. They ask things like "How has this issue impacted you?" or "What do *you* think is the best way to solve this challenge?"

Their body language also conveys a greater depth of listening. While mediocre reps are typically listening for opportunity, superstars listen for true understanding. You can often tell that more mediocre reps are often just waiting for the other person to finish, because their physical presence gives off a vibe of impatience.

Another seemingly subtle yet hugely important difference between the superstars and their less successful counterparts is the order in which they present their information. Less successful people often lead with their own information, and then ask their customers what they think of it.

Superstars ask questions about the customer's situation first, then share their information. Now remember, in many instances all the reps from a given company are showing the exact same data. So it's not like the superstars can truly customize their presentations. They don't share different information; they just share it in a different order.

The simple act of asking questions, and actually listening to the answers, before they deliver their message, dramatically improves the customer's response.

It's also worth noting that average salespeople often spend a lot of time handling customer objections and obstacles after they've given their pitch. Superstars encounter far fewer obstacles because they uncover all that information before they start sharing.

Superstar performers demonstrate that if we're serious about holding a space for the other person's perspective, we need to proactively find out what that perspective is.

▶ What might happen if you asked your coworker or boss what their goals for the company or department were before you started telling them what you thought should be done?

▶ What would happen if you asked your conservative or liberal neighbor what their hopes were for your community or country before you shared your opinion?

▶ How might your in-laws respond if you asked them what they thought was important about disciplining children before giving them your rules about building self-esteem?

▶ How might it affect your marriage if you asked your spouse how you could show more love to them, before you told them the ways they need to show more love to you?

It helps if you actually care about the answer, but sometimes the act of asking the questions is enough to start the process.

Interesting Versus Interested

Asking good questions is a common theme among all top performers in every field; in fact, I've noticed that sometimes it's hard to keep them from asking questions.

Whenever I'm working with a client, I try to keep the experience focused on them. So beyond a short intro and some small talk to make people feel comfortable, the conversation is about their needs and goals. But this is frequently challenging with top performers. They're so interested in new people and new ideas that they're curious about everything, including me.

In many cases, I've had the experience of getting into the car with a salesperson I'd never met prior to them picking me up at the airport or hotel, and having them tell me, "Oh wow, I Googled you, can you tell me about your books, I'm particularly interested in this one." Or "I read your column about love and leadership. How did you come up with that model?"

They also ask the waitress where she got her earrings, and the cab driver how long he's been driving, and the hotel clerk if they're having a good day.

Middle-of-the-pack performers ask far fewer questions of others. They may try every trick in the book to make themselves seem more *interesting*, but the top performers are always sincerely *interested*.

If you're wondering whether you're one of the superstars or one of the average folks, you might want to ask yourself how much you know about the people you deal with on a daily basis. If there are a lot of gaps, you might want to reread the previous section on questions or download "10 Great Questions to Ask Your Spouse, Coworker, or Prospect" off our site before your next interaction.

Who's Afraid to Let the Other Guy Talk?

Superstars are fascinated by new people and ideas because their minds aren't stuck on their own agendas. While their lesser-performing counterparts are frequently bogged down by a subtle self-imposed worry track, superstars are eager to find out about everybody else.

I say *subtle* because it's not that most of us are quaking in our boots every minute at the thought of potential failure. But when you're primarily concerned about your own agenda, it becomes the overriding theme of your brain chatter.

When people struggle to get others to go along with their plans, it's often because they don't have a place to safely house their agenda, so it dominates their thinking. Their thoughts about what they want to happen or what they plan to say wind up sitting smack between them and the person they're trying to connect with. Superstars have no such barriers. When they're with you, they're totally with you, which is what we all want from our interactions, because it brings out the best in everyone.

Some people are naturally better at it than others, and can more easily assimilate both sides of the Triangle. But that doesn't mean the rest of us are destined to be single-agenda bottom fishers forever.

We've all probably had experiences where we came into situations as our best self, and we seamlessly connected with other people and everything seemed to go our way. We just need to remember what that feels like and do more of it.

It's usually just when we're stressed or anxious that we revert back to our either/or brains, and we forget to hold a space for the other person.

It breaks my heart to think about how many times my kids or husband have been speaking, and I've been just waiting for them to finish, so that I can tell them what we really need to do. It's not that I don't love them, but when I'm busy or rushed, I'm more inclined to focus on the path I think is important.

Going down the path we're most comfortable with is why politicians create polarization, and why men and women argue about sex and communication. We're all just trying to further an agenda that we believe works. And we're often so well-versed in our own information that all our interactions are organized around sharing what we know, and suggesting solutions based on our own perspective alone.

But the lessons from sales are simple:

- ▸ Top performers show up with love and help other people accomplish their goals.

- ▸ Mediocre performers view other people as a means to accomplish their own goals.

Mediocre salespeople aren't bad people. There have been several times in my life when I've been one of them. They're only guilty of making the same mistake we all make when we're afraid we're not going to get our way. They forget to hold a space for the other person's perspective.

And, like many of us, when they hear something that might derail them from the path they want to go down, or that might cause conflict, they often develop a bad case of the "Yes, buts."

This is a problem that plagues us all, and not just in business. It often shows up in our most intimate relationships.

Why Love Means
Never Having to Say, "Yes, But"

I once saw a *Dr. Phil* show featuring a couple trying to repair their marriage after the husband's affair. (Even if you're not a fan of Dr. Phil hang in here with me; there's a point that applies to business, politics, religion, and even your narrow-minded neighbor.)

The husband had an affair, and although he had apologized, come back to his family, and was clearly incredibly regretful over his mistake, the wife was having a hard time letting go of it. She kept rehashing it over, and over, and over again.

As she reiterated the obviously well-trod ground of "You don't know how much you hurt me," the husband looked contrite for a while. But he eventually got frustrated listening to something he had obviously heard a thousand times over, and he responded with, "Yes, I know, but it happened over a year ago. Can't we just put it behind us and move on?

Enter Dr. Phil, who wisely told the man, "A woman can't move on until she feels heard."

Up until that point the husband had said he was sorry many times, and he had done everything he could to make amends. But he had never really validated her feelings.

While she kept telling him how awful it felt, he kept apologizing and telling her that it hadn't meant a thing.

His words might have been, "Let's move on, it didn't mean anything." But she probably heard, "Your feelings are no big deal, let's just forget about it."

Again, it's thoughts of love versus thoughts of fear. With his personal life splayed out on national television I have no doubt that the poor man was probably terrified. What man in his right mind would want to further encourage his wife to talk about his failings? On TV. With Dr. Phil.

However, with Dr. Phil coaching him along, the courageous husband was finally able to say, "It must have felt like you had been punched in the stomach. Like I had kicked you to the curb and stomped on your heart."

From the moment the words left his mouth, you could see his wife's tensed-up shoulders begin to soften, the wall of anger surrounding her melted into sadness as the cameras continued to roll.

The husband went on to say, "All this time I've been asking you to forgive me, but what you really wanted was for me to know how you feel."

In that one marriage-changing moment, she finally felt heard. The tension left her body, she exhaled in relief, and just like that, *poof,* the self-erected barrier of angst between them was gone.

I'm sure she still carried the sadness, but once she knew that he understood where she was coming from, she was ready to move to higher ground.

So how does this relate to getting what you want from your spouse or boss and the Triangle of Truth?

The injured wife is a dramatic example of how quickly you can change the energy of a conflict, disagreement, or even a contentious neighborhood party, by simply validating the other person's perspective.

When the husband went into his "yes, buts" it seemed to his wife that he wasn't really listening. He was trying to avoid dealing with her emotions in the hopes that they could simply move on.

In his defense, he was probably reluctant to give voice to his wife's hurt feelings; who wants to face the pain of breaking the heart of the woman they love? However, unfortunately for him, ignoring the wife's feelings just made her feel more hurt, a hurt that translated into simmering anger and resentment. Anger and resentment that had probably spilled out onto the husband every single day since his wife discovered his cheating. (Doesn't *that* sound like a fun way to live?)

What's interesting here is that the husband probably thought he was dealing with her feelings all along. In fact, he probably thought he was having to deal with them all the time—that's why he was apologizing all over the place. But for her, apologizing and understanding were two different things. Until she heard him say the words that described exactly the way she felt, she couldn't let it go.

If you're a man and you're rolling your eyes right now thinking, "Great. Just what I need, yet another woman telling me I need to better understand someone's feelings," take a deep breath. I chose this example for very specific reasons.

Most of us can relate to this all too common scenario inside an intimate relationship, and sometimes seeing an exaggerated version of something helps us spot the same dynamic when it shows up in our own lives.

I've also seen similar scenarios play out in business settings, parent–teacher conferences, community meetings, and on the world stage. It's not limited to male–female interactions. I've been in executive sessions where two men's failure to validate each other created such anger that the entire meeting threatened to come to blows.

The *Dr. Phil* couple weren't tearing each other apart physically, but they certainly were emotionally. They had been rehashing this awful thing for over a year, with the husband continually apologizing, and the wife still angry. It had gotten them nowhere.

However, the moment the husband finally validated her feelings, the entire dynamic changed.

If you're a woman reading this, and you're thinking, "I need to show this part to my husband so that he will finally see how important it is to understand my emotions," hold up, honey. I'm with you, and I've been just as frustrated with my husband's discomfort with my emotions as the next woman, but I'll also tell you that while we women usually want our partner to acknowledge our emotions, men have an equally strong, and equally valid, need to have their actions, work, and tasks acknowledged.

When we don't notice or acknowledge the things they do, it's just as painful for them as it is for us when they don't notice or acknowledge the way we feel.

If you've ever had the "Why don't you care how I feel?" versus "Why don't you notice what I do?" argument, you know what I'm talking about.

It doesn't always play out along these stereotypical gender divisions. But if you find yourself asking for your partner to notice one thing, while they keep asking you to notice another, you might want to just try validating whatever it is they're asking you for.

Yes, I know, you probably feel they should validate your side first. But as the examples of sales reps and the apologizing husband demonstrate, the best way to get people to go along with your agenda is to demonstrate that you care about theirs.

Therein lies the Triangle of Truth lesson. It's not enough to *think* you understand the person on the other side, you have to

> It's not enough to *think* you understand the person on the other side; you have to *show* that you do.

show that you do. The moment that the other side sees that you truly understand their perspective is the moment they finally begin to believe that you are fully informed. It is only then when they're confident that you hear their side that they can begin to hear yours.

How many times have you found yourself saying or thinking, "They just don't get it." Frustrating, isn't it? You explain yourself time and time again, yet they still don't seem to understand. We've all been there.

But let me ask you this, how likely are you to want to work with, cooperate with, or, dare I say, sleep with, someone who doesn't really understand you? You may do it, and in the case of sex, you might even enjoy it. But it's never going to be as productive or satisfying as it would be if you were truly connected to the other person.

It's easier for them to connect with you if you make the effort to connect with them. And the way you connect is not just by sharing yourself, but by holding a space for the other person to share themselves.

I want to make an important distinction here: Understanding someone doesn't necessarily mean agreeing with them. The wife may have been thinking, "What you did to me was worse than eating your own young. You should be shot at dawn with everyone in this audience watching and cheering." The husband didn't have to validate her assessment of his character or agree with her imagined action plan. All he had to do was show her that he heard her pain.

It doesn't matter whether you're married to the person, or you're trying to sell to them, or you're trying to hammer out legislation to save the planet with them, they have thoughts and feelings that are different from yours. They have different ideas about what the problems are, and different ideas about how to solve them. You can try to understand their perspective, or you can ignore it. But their thoughts, needs, goals, and emotions aren't going to go away.

When you make an effort to understand the other person's core truths, and validate them, things can change more quickly than you might imagine.

It helps if you really mean it, but this is one of those instances where faking it until you make it really does work.

Act As If

Many of us have heard the expression, act as if. If you want to be successful, act as if you already are. If you want to be the best speaker on the planet, pretend you're there right now. If you want to be an organized person, act like you were born clutching a Franklin Planner. If you want to be a more loving spouse, act as if you already are.

It might seem disingenuous or inauthentic to pretend to be something that you're not, particularly when it comes to feelings. Why should we act as though we like someone, or care about them, or respect them, when we really don't?

I'd be the last person to tell you to stuff your feelings. But if you *want to* feel a certain way, acting like you already do can get you to a place where the feeling become genuine.

Our mind, body, spirit interface expert Dr. Strozzi-Heckler suggests that rather than thinking of it as faking it, think of it as practice.

▶ If I want to care more about my spouse's perspective, the next time he or she talks, I'm going to practice acting like I do.

▶ If I want to be more empathetic to my coworkers' agendas, in the next meeting, I'm going to practice behaving like a person who actually does listen.

If you practice with your body, which includes your mouth and your mind, your spirit will eventually follow. Strozzi-Heckler has found that:

▶ Three hundred repetitions of an action establishes a muscle memory

▶ After three thousand repetitions, the action becomes part of who you are

There's not a parent alive who hasn't pretended to be patient when they were feeling anything but. If you do it enough times, you actually become the patient parent that you want to be.

One of the reasons the "fake it till you make it, practice till you feel it" model works is because it's self-reinforcing. You do it and you feel better, and after a time or two, or three thousand, someone responds in a more positive way, and it reinforces the validity of your approach.

For the record, when it comes to holding a space for the other person's agenda I'm probably at three thousand repetitions with my clients and kids, and it really is part of who I am. But I've probably barely cracked three hundred with my husband. Which means I know what it feels like, but it's not always my natural inclination.

However, I remain hopeful that with about 2,700 more practice sessions, I will indeed become a superstar spouse.

Can I Get a Witness?

As human beings, we have a fundamental need to be seen. That's why little kids shout, "Look at me, Mom, look at me." It's as though going off the high dive doesn't count unless someone sees you do it.

We have an innate need for other people to know who we are and what we're about. We need other people to witness our lives: our joy, our pain, our sadness, our accomplishments, our goals, and our dreams. There is nothing so glorious as being with a person who truly sees you, and who thinks you're fabulous.

> We have an innate need for other people to know who we are and what we're about.

When someone notices us they validate our existence. We feel seen and heard, and we feel happy. When we feel ignored, we find ourselves descending into anger and hurt. The number one complaint couples usually have with each other is "he or she doesn't understand me," and worse, they don't even try to. Unspoken and misunderstood feelings keep us stuck in almost every area of our lives.

When we view others as obstacles to getting what we want, or even as helpers who can aid us, we're not truly seeing them. Is it any wonder we can't create peace with others, or marry our plans and goals with others when our version of success is often a one-sided agenda?

The Triangle model enables you to hold a place for the other person's agenda without giving up your own—even if it's not your natural inclination to do so. By making a decision to consciously put your own thoughts on pause, you open a space for the other person to step into. Because when you make the decision to show up with openness and love, other people instinctively respond in kind.

But we don't have to wait until we start feeling loving emotions to begin the process. The way we create loving emotions is by thinking loving thoughts. It really is that simple.

When you come from a place of love, you're not inclined to blow past other people's thoughts and feelings; you strive to truly understand them. You hold them in your heart as well as your mind, and their side of the Triangle becomes just as important as yours.

Love expands our opportunities, while fear contracts them.

Whether it's the fear that things might not work out the way we planned or that other people will take advantage or simply that we'll look foolish, fear is the unseen barrier that separates us from each other. It can be as dramatic as a screaming spouse or as subtle as a sales rep worried about making bonus. When our brains are on the fear track, we tend to ignore the thoughts and feelings of others. Our minds have descended into either/or, and all we're focused on is our own perspective

It is by holding a space for others that we open ourselves up to the possibility of *And*.

But if we want to make the shift, all we have to do is change our thoughts. Instead of allowing our ego to constantly reinforce fear-based, self-serving thoughts, we can choose love-based thoughts of co-creating. Instead of worrying that we might not get our way, or that our agenda may be in peril, we can make a conscious decision to open up a space for thoughts and feelings of others.

It is by holding a space for others that we open ourselves up to the possibility of *And*.

As every superstar knows, you don't have to pick between their agenda and your agenda: The fastest route to top of the Triangle is to assimilate both.

Seek Higher Ground

*How to Rise Above the Comfort and
Convenience of False Choices*

For here we are not afraid to follow the truth,
wherever it may lead.
—THOMAS JEFFERSON

"Lisa, you're going to have to make a decision.

It's a difficult choice and I encourage you to talk it over with your husband. This is something you need to decide as a couple. Ultimately, you two are the only ones who can decide what's best for you.

However, we have a short window of time here, and you're going to have to let me know within the next few weeks."

Believe it or not, this was a career counseling session with a well-intentioned boss who was trying to help me decide whether or not to take a transfer.

I was twenty-five years old and worked for a consumer products company. I had worked my way up to the highly coveted position of midlevel sales manager, and we were talking about where I might go from there. Looking back, it's probably more accurate to say that I was clinging to the bottom rung of middle management, hoping that perhaps the big boys in charge would see greatness in my future. Fortunately for me, they thought I had potential.

The trouble was, greatness didn't seem to be available in Atlanta, where I currently resided. If I wanted to get promoted I was going to have to move. They weren't sure where, but they needed to know if I was willing to do it when the opportunity came up.

In the pool of other wannabe executives, I was one of the few who had a husband. There were several married men, but not many married women.

The single people could just pack up and go, and most of the married guys had wives who, while they might not have been clamoring to trek across the country for their husband's job, were certainly willing to do it for the sake of advancement.

And then there was my spouse. A man nine years older than me who was less than enthused about quitting his job and moving to a yet-to-be-determined location, where we would know no one, in order for me to take a position that paid less than the one I was asking him to quit. Go figure.

So I went in for the "big talk." The division manager was truly a nice guy, and I knew that he liked me and wanted the best for me. But here's what he said:

"Lisa, you have to make a choice. You need to decide whether it's going to be your career or his. One of you is going to have to take a backseat. In my family, we decided that my career would come first and hers would be second. We've been married for twenty years and it worked out for us. I can't tell you which one of you it should be, but between the two of you, you're going to have to decide whose career comes first."

Before you jump to the conclusion that the guy was sexist, let me tell you, I believed then, and I believe now, that he was a kind man, a long-married husband and father who had daughters himself. True, he probably wasn't having this conversation with any of the male go-getters. But none of them had ever told him that moving might be a problem.

I felt like I was being asked to script the future of my entire life at the age of twenty-five. The way he posed the question made me feel as though once the decision was made, it was going to be that way forever.

I'm embarrassed to admit it, but my first thought was something along the lines of, "If somebody is going to be lead dog, it's going to be me." I wasn't working sixty hours a week to play second fiddle to a man, even if he was my husband.

Did I mention that my company sold deodorant and toilet paper? And that the potential promotion would catapult me from the bottom rung of middle management squarely into the middle of middle management? What person in their right mind wouldn't ask their spouse to take a backseat for that kind of glamour?

For once, the filter between my brain and my mouth was actually working. I kept my self-absorbed thoughts to myself and told the boss that my husband and I would talk about it over the weekend and I would get back to him next week.

On the way home that day, I had an hour in traffic to think. As I sat in my powder blue K car, my stout-heeled navy blue pumps kicked to the floorboard, my little red bow tie and my boxy navy pinstripe jacket thrown across the baby blue velour bench seat, the traffic was so heavy that it was stop and go the whole way. Tense as I was, my foot was moving so jerkily back and forth between the brake and the gas that the dark brown reinforced toe of my suntan control-top panty hose was now black, and the cases of deodorant samples and triplicate call report forms that had been carefully organized in the backseat were now spilling all over each other. (It was the 1980s, and I was in outside sales.)

As I thought about the situation, I contemplated creating a spreadsheet outlining my five-year earning potential in the hopes that I could convince my husband that we should take a transfer to God knows where so that I could further my climb up the corporate ladder.

However, in a moment of uncharacteristic maturity I began to think about this from my husband's perspective. Yes my career was important, but I doubt he was waking up and going to work each day because he considered his job a hobby. It didn't seem fair to ask him to take a backseat, when I didn't want to take one.

It was at that moment that I realized that my boss was asking the wrong question.

Asking me to decide whose career came first is like telling a parent, you have two kids, but you only have the money to send one to college, which one do you choose? Duh! The answer is both, and we figure out a way to make it work: They go part-time, they take turns, we get loans. Both kids are equally important so you figure out a way to make it work as a family.

My boss may have been well-intentioned, but he was operating from an either/or paradigm—a model that had been accepted for years, but one that was nonetheless limiting to all parties involved.

I know many families prioritize one career over the other, and I'm not making any suggestions as to how you should earn your paycheck. But when you set up a dynamic that forces people to choose one important thing over another important thing, you often lose sight of your real goals.

It happens in many situations, because it's the status quo or we're too stressed, worried, or uncreative to envision how we might do things differently.

In this particular situation, we decided that neither career came first. Our marriage did. It certainly would have been easier for everyone if we could have just scripted it all out right then and there at the start of our lives. I would know my place, my husband would know his, and the company would know whether I should be on the fast track, or if I was going to stay a midlevel flunky until the day I keeled over, head down on an expense report.

There are certain situations where we do have to prioritize one thing over another. However, in many cases, we succumb to false choices simply because it's quicker and easier, for everyone. Our unwillingness to tolerate ambiguity rears its ugly head again.

Life may be simpler when you pass out roles, put people into categories, and expect them to stay "in character" forever, but the false choices stifle our thinking about ourselves, and our organizations.

Whether it's assuming that our government has to choose between giving people freedom or demanding responsibility, or that our households must be either disciplined or creative, whenever we err on one side at the exclusion of another, we limit ourselves.

In the case of the dueling careers, even though my well-intended boss was presenting it as either your career or your husband's, we decided that making a forever decision at that stage of our marriage didn't make sense. Instead of choosing one path or the other, we decided that we were going to take opportunities on a case by case basis, and that our criteria would be what was best for our family, and our own personal growth.

As it turns out, doing some deep thinking about what was best for our marriage, and what was best for my own growth as a human being, led me to the conclusion that perhaps becoming the Queen of Consumer Products wasn't the best path for me. I wound up leaving the company a year later to take a job with a sales training firm, where I learned skills that eventually launched my career as a writer and speaker. I never would have discovered those opportunities had I stayed stuck in the two choices that were being presented.

Sometimes human beings, however well-intended, can only see limited options, whether it's because that's what we're being presented with or because that's the way things have always been done.

But if we can discipline ourselves to be still for a moment and not react, we can expand our thinking. Sometimes that means asking different questions than the ones currently being posed to you, and sometimes that means sitting in traffic with the radio off so that you can think about what you really want in life.

Fortunately for me, my early career contemplation moment took place before everyone had cell phones and when company cars only had AM radios. (Yes, young readers, there was such a time, and it wasn't *that* long ago.)

Would I have reached similar conclusions if I had my email-sending iPhone or music library at my disposal? Perhaps. I like to imagine that I would have put on some soft music, gotten myself into a state of calm, and pondered big thoughts about the true meaning of my life and what I really wanted for myself. But given that I later spent much of my thirties frantically yammering into a cell phone, it's probably a good thing I didn't have many options back then.

Disciplining myself to think about the bigger picture and consider the full context of situations is something I continually have to remind myself to do. But if we can train our brains to look behind the presenting choices, we can make smarter decisions. Instead of simply trying to decide which is more important, option A or option B, we need to step back, and ask ourselves *what we really want.*

It's hard to know if you're moving toward your goals, especially if you haven't clarified them. And even if you have clarified your objectives, you often find yourself so mired in the daily grind, it's easy to forget what we really wanted to accomplish in the first place.

The busyness of our lives, our categorizing brains, and our discomfort with uncertain outcomes, all prompt us to short-circuit the challenging process of co-creating.

Either/or thinking doesn't just happen when we're afraid; it's a shortcut we use in many situations.

The media frequently helps us along in our either/or false choices mind-set by perpetuating the "two simple sides to everything" model, particularly in politics or public debate. Nuanced discussion is lost, as we're treated to a split screen of two people arguing complex issues in sound bite format, implying to the viewers that there are only these two choices.

But it's not just the systems surrounding us that prompt us to create false choices; we also frequently create them ourselves because we're unwilling or unable to elevate our own minds and sort through the challenging process of creating something different.

Think about it; which is harder, building a government around the seemingly competing concepts of freedom and responsibility or just choosing one of those two values and creating a system that supports that alone?

That was one of the dilemmas facing Thomas Jefferson and John Adams back in 1776, and I, for one, am certainly glad they opted to create a new path.

We Hold These Truths to Be Complementary

John Adams, considered by most historians to be a conservative, and Thomas Jefferson, whom most viewed as a liberal, were the two men primarily responsible for writing and presenting the Declaration of Independence.

They didn't have much time, and with Ben Franklin ill, Adams, as the next senior statesman in line, got the job of writing it. However, he suggested that Jefferson should be the primary writer, saying, "You're ten times the writer I am." Jefferson reluctantly agreed.

But eloquent writer that he was, Jefferson wasn't a great speaker. So it was decided that Adams, who was known for his outstanding oratory, should occupy the foremost position in the debate on its adoption. It was Adams who defended it before the Continental Congress on July 2. He must have done a good job, because they approved it two days later on July 4, 1776.

The Declaration of Independence is one of history's finest examples of how truths that were once considered to be conflicting can combine to create a whole that is greater than the sum of its parts. The role that Jefferson and Adams played in creating it holds lessons that apply to this day.

Jefferson, an advocate for freedom of thought, and Adams, a staunch believer in the rule of law, were unlikely allies. Yet can you imagine where our country might be had we not had both their perspectives during our creation? Some might believe that we would better off if only one voice had prevailed. Yet it was Jefferson and Adams's combination of the ideals that created a nation that now affords us the freedom to argue over which man was right.

Espousing seemingly competing ideals, ideals that many suggest represent the roots of this country's liberal versus conservative debates, Jefferson and Adams came together in that one shining moment to create something that was bigger than anything either of them could have envisioned alone. They were willing to do the hard work of co-creating because they loved their new country too much to short-circuit their thinking.

They didn't put their lives on the line to settle for the comfort or convenience of false choices. They weren't going to choose between their ideals; they were going to combine them.

The Myth of the Middle Ground

Many people believe that compromise is the best way to solve their problems. I'm all about trying to create a path that we can agree on, and I'd be the last person to suggest that we shouldn't sit down and try to work out our disagreements.

But I think in many cases, we succumb to compromise because we lack the creativity to see how our perspectives can be merged without watering them down. So we both give up a little of what we want in the hopes that we can meet in the middle to create a solution that includes at least some of what we originally really wanted. And it works, sort of. But if you talk to anyone who's ever given up their dream for the sake of the greater good, you know that there can be bitter aftereffects.

- ► People make budget concessions and then forever begrudge the other party every nickel they spend.

- ► Spouses put their own career on hold to support the other person and then resent it when their partner becomes more successful.

- ► Community leaders compromise in order to get something done but then wind up belittling the project because they don't really believe in some of the components.

The more aggressive solution is to negotiate. I've taught sales seminars for years, and I used to teach traditional negotiating tactics. Here's the way it usually works. You find out what they really want without revealing what you really want. You then give them something of low value to you, but of high-perceived value to them. You do this with the intent of lulling them into thinking they just got something good, which you can then use as leverage to get them to cough up what you really want.

But here's the problem with that model. If you're a skilled negotiator, you don't give up anything really important, you just make the other guy *think* you gave up something important, so that he will give up something really good. We call it win/win. But if we're honest, the mind-set is really I win, you think you won. And while you may leave feeling satisfied, the other guy often isn't.

If you're a less skilled negotiator you find yourself putting things on the table that you probably shouldn't, and you wind up feeling not very good about the deal after it has closed, especially if you have to explain it to your spouse or boss, or you discover that you could have gotten more and given less.

People say that life is about compromise, or you get what you negotiate. It's also been said that a good legal decision is one that leaves both sides unhappy. But is that really how we want to live—always assuming that we either have to give in to the other guy, or outmaneuver him?

Both approaches—the concessions of compromise and the hardball tactics of negotiation—are predicated on the paradigm that our views are incompatible. There may be times when compromise or negotiation are appropriate, but if we approach every potential conflict with the assumption that someone is going to have to give in, that's exactly what will happen, and giving in rarely puts us on a path toward creating greatness.

Either/or thinking locks us into the land of false choices. Past experience and one-dimensional perspectives cause us to believe that our ideals are somehow incompatible with those of the person on the other side of the triangle, so we believe that our only choice is either to cave in or to hammer the other side for concessions.

Sometimes we do need to give a little to get a little. But I think in many cases what we actually need to give is more thought to how our ideals can be leveraged into something bigger, rather than watering them down for the sake of a quick agreement or stonewalling and manipulating people until we get what we want.

Whether we call it compromise or negotiation, diluting our ideals or making tit-for-tat exchanges never works over the long haul, because the emphasis is on whittling down one or both parties. It might be appropriate for onetime interaction on the used car lot, but it doesn't create an environment that will sustain success or unite us in a greater purpose.

If we truly want to create great companies, countries, communities, families, and relationships, we need to change our paradigm.

Instead of approaching situations believing that we must choose between either being the strong person who holds her ground or the kind person who is willing to move the middle ground, we need to start seeking higher ground.

We don't have to make a choice between being strong and being kind. We can be both, and in doing so we can achieve greatness in the grand tradition of Thomas Jefferson and John Adams.

Buddhism refers to it as the Middle Way. It doesn't mean a compromise between your way and my way; it means a higher way, a path that we can create together.

We don't have to choose between holding ground or the middle ground; we can decide to co-create a path to the high ground.

Like Jefferson and Adams, there will be times when our commitment to our ideals enables us to come together beautifully. There will also be times when our commitment to certain truths causes us to argue and fight. But if we continue to aim for the top of the Triangle, and stay committed to something larger than ourselves, we will continue to elevate the conversation.

> We don't have to choose between holding ground or the middle ground; we can decide to co-create a path to the high ground.

The Bumpy Path to Greatness

If you're a history buff, you know that in the years that followed their collaboration on the Declaration of Independence, Jefferson and Adams's political differences frequently put them at odds, and for many years they were bitter rivals.

During his two terms as vice president under George Washington, Adams had frequent conflicts with then secretary of state Jefferson. Adams went on to become the second president after narrowly beating out Jefferson. Four years later, Jefferson became the third president, after upsetting Adams's bid for a second term. Adams was so angry he left town and didn't even attend the inauguration.

Did their differences make their lives easier? Hardly. I'm sure there were times when they each wished the other would just shut up. But, in June and July of 1776, they were smart enough to know that while forcing a choice between seemingly competing ideas might feel quicker and easier, it rarely results in greatness.

The differing ideals that made the Declaration of Independence great and pitted Jefferson and Adams against each other for most of their political careers were the very same ideals that they continued to debate via letters when they resumed their relationship later in life. After their careers were over, their mutual friend, peacemaker Dr. Benjamin Rush, suggested that they begin corresponding again.

The letters the two men exchanged in their later years reveal that while they still frequently disagreed, they also admired each other's intellects. I guess this demonstrates that while differences may drive us apart, when you come at them from a place of common purpose and have the benefit of maturity, you recognize the value of what the other side is saying.

Jefferson and Adams continued their synergistic push/pull relationship even in death. In a you-can't-make-this-up, history-meets-divine-intervention moment, both men died on the same day, the fourth of July. Jefferson passed first and then Adams. On July 4, 1826, exactly fifty years to the day of the birth of the country they founded, each man passed away without even knowing that his longtime co-creator and nemesis was facing his demise as well.

They died within hours of each other. Rumor has it that the messenger dispatched to Jefferson's home to carry the news of Adams's death passed the messenger who had been sent to Adams's home to inform him of Jefferson's death.

Jefferson and Adams are the embodiment of the Triangle of

Truth because they didn't succumb to false choices. Their goal was to create something new and different, and they were open to assimilating each other's ideas. They didn't allow themselves to descend into either/or thinking because they had already experienced the perils of one-dimensional rule, and they were determined that everyone should have a voice.

Their love for their emerging country and their respect for each other enabled them to put the full power of their formidable intellects into creating something that few had ever even dreamed possible.

Yet as smart as they both were, they didn't allow their egos to take over. If you think about Adams asking Jefferson to write the Declaration, when he could have done it himself, and many thought he should, you see a man who cares more about creating something amazing than he does about getting his own way. When you think about Jefferson handing over the biggest work of his life to Adams, and allowing him to present it, you see a man who knows his own talents and puts them into service, yet who knows when it's time to get help from someone who is better at something than he is.

Jefferson and Adams didn't get everything right. Slavery and not allowing women to vote are the two errors in judgment that most readily spring to mind, but remember the flawed and fabulous nature of human beings? These were great men, but they weren't above making mistakes. We needn't let their narrow thinking about some issues negate their great thinking about others. It just reminds us that we all have our blind spots and that our values spring as much from our environments as they do from our brains.

Our forefathers didn't create this country with the intention that we would stay stagnant. Our job is to take what they did and build on it. If they didn't get everything right on the first round, we can fix it. But the best way to improve upon their work is to embody the same kind of high-level thinking they employed when they created this nation.

The lessons of the Jefferson and Adams collaboration are many, and they apply to more than just our government; they apply to everything we do.

- ► How many times have we stifled outcomes because we couldn't hear what our rival had to say?

- ► How often have we succumbed to false choices because we were unwilling to take the time to co-create?

- ► How frequently do we convince ourselves that we have to choose one of two paths because we can't see an easy way to assimilate them?

- ► And how many times has our ego told us that an idea is wrong, therefore, the people promoting it don't deserve a voice?

The "Therefore" Trap

We fall into the "therefore" trap when we're trying to prove ourselves right and make sure that our ideas come out on top. Our minds tell us that we need to speed up a discussion so that we can get to the solution (our solution) more quickly.

"This is my truth; therefore, this is what we should do about it."

It's when our egos are working overtime behind the scenes

to help our minds discount the thoughts and opinions of other people. "They said this; therefore, it must mean that they are total losers; and therefore, we should ignore everything they say."

The "therefore" trap is a mental shortcut our mind takes in order to prevent us from having to tolerate the ambiguity of an uncertain outcome. It's kind of a cool trick: we get to avoid ambiguity and prove ourselves right at the same time. Gosh, we're smart.

Have you ever heard or said any of these?

- ► The people in data processing don't support operations; therefore, they don't really care about this company.

- ► My in-laws are always trying to get me to do things their way; therefore, they have no respect for me.

- ► They're liberals; therefore, they don't care about traditional values.

- ► They're conservatives; therefore, they don't care about the poor.

- ► She's always so tied up in the minutia; therefore, she must not see the big picture.

- ► He always has his head in the clouds; therefore, he doesn't know what goes on day to day.

- ► My spouse never wants to talk; therefore, he or she doesn't love me.

- ► My kids are always whining; therefore, they don't appreciate anything I do.

▶ My neighbor gave me a dirty look; therefore, she must not like me.

The "therefore" trap effectively halts any type of creative thinking and keeps us stuck on one side of the line. And it happens in a multitude of situations.

> **The "therefore" trap halts creative thinking and keeps us stuck on one side of the line.**

An example of how this can play out in a business setting is the case of the consumer electronics giant Best Buy. When then senior vice president Julie Gilbert began rolling out an initiative to improve the shopping experience for women, many of the male store personnel initially resisted. Gilbert says, "They thought we were going to ruin the Best Buy experience for men."

Many of the men assumed, "They want to improve the stores for women; therefore, it will be a less great experience for men." Some even wondered aloud if the big-screen-TV-and-video-game–selling Best Buy stores would be painted pink.

However, as the WOLF initiative (now a trademarked innovation process) rolled out, it became obvious that improving the stores for women also improved the stores for men. Gilbert says one of the ways she was able to sell the initiative was to role-play for the stores how a man's apartment often improves when he gets a girlfriend. "She cleans the scum off the bathroom, she gets some nice furniture, she puts some pictures on the wall, and suddenly the man is enjoying his own space more."

Five years later, the results of Best Buy being willing to rise above either/or thinking to embrace *And* speak for themselves.

By improving their stores through the eyes of women (and no, they're not pink; they're still blue), Best Buy increased their female revenue by $4.4 billion, female market share increased from 14.7 to 17.1 percent, *And* they improved sales and customer retention with male consumers. (Read "How Best Buy Rose Above Either/Or and Made $4 Billion" on our site.)

We often disconnect our business experiences from our personal experiences. But the either/or thinking that prompted many of the men at Best Buy to initially resist making the stores better for women, believing that the stores could either cater to men or women, but not both, is the very same either/or thinking that prompts us to succumb to false choices on many fronts. In the Best Buy scenario it was men, but we women do exactly the same thing if we feel that something we like is being threatened.

Crossovers: Problematic and Successful (Sometimes)

False choices make life easier. Or at least they seem to.

Not just for us, but for everyone. Think about how simple life would be if we all walked around with labels on our foreheads—pro-gun, pro-immigration, pro-choice, pro-life. What if that one word told you everything you needed to know about a person. How simple would that be? We would hardly have to think at all. The world would be so ordered and neat, and we would know how to respond to everything.

The truth is, we like to put people and ideas into categories and slap labels on them because we don't like to think. Well, actually we do like to think. Sort of. We like to brood, we like to fantasize, we like to complain, we like to whine, we like to make judgments, we like to think about how we can get our way, and we like for other people to think so that we can tell them whether their ideas are right or wrong.

However, we often resist doing conceptual high-level thinking ourselves. Again, not because we're evil, but because it's hard, and we don't have time to contemplate every little thing.

That's why music and bookstores create categories, so that we don't have to process through every single item or scour the entire store to find what we're looking for. We can just go to the section we like.

Categories themselves aren't a bad thing, but if we always allow other people to define them for us, we may be cheating ourselves out of creating something great.

It's no coincidence that in the music business many of the biggest breakout acts have been crossover artists. Elvis, of course, was the ultimate crossover, creating a musical revolution with his swivel hips and curling lip. But rock operas, country pop duets, Christian rock, and classical pop are all examples of creatives who thought beyond the existing categories and didn't allow themselves to be confined by false choices.

Of course, redefining the categories doesn't always make life easier for the people who created them. Would you want to be the stock clerk who had to figure out where to put the Dolly Parton–Smokey Robinson duet? (Yes, they did make one.)

But sometimes trying to move out of your assigned category does more than upset the people who created the categories; sometimes it upsets everyone. Garth Brooks certainly learned that lesson.

Why John Adams Sold
the Declaration, but Garth
Brooks Couldn't Sell Chris Gaines

In 1999, the cowboy-hat-wearing, platinum-record-selling country music superstar Garth Brooks took a walk on the wild side and recorded an alternative rock album. He recorded under the name Chris Gaines, a fictional character he was slated to play in a movie. The music was a totally different style, more of an R & B feel, and Garth even adopted a new persona for the CD jacket. Gone were the jeans, boots, big belt buckle, and country boy grin. As Gaines, he sported fringy hair, a mod black-and-white striped shirt, and one of those little tuft beardlike things in the center of his chin, you know, the kind that poetry-reading twenty-somethings often sport. It was a total departure from the good old boy Garth's millions of fans had come to know and love.

You would have thought Rush Limbaugh and Gloria Steinem had just announced that they were engaged. The fans went nuts—and not in a good way. They felt betrayed.

They were totally unreceptive to the idea of Garth being anything other than their country guy who belted out songs about the highs and lows of love and rodeos.

Professional music critics admired Brooks for taking a risk, but his fans were downright angry. I read one article quoting a fan saying, "Garth Brooks has turned his back on the people who made him famous, and I'm not going to forgive him for this."

I swear, I'm not making this up. People were that mad. Garth's fans were seethingly angry that a creative genius had the audacity to venture outside the category they had placed him in.

Keep in mind, Garth Brooks is one of the bestselling artists of all time, second only to the Beatles in the United States. He has sold millions of albums, and ironically enough, he was already one of country's most successful crossover artists. A powerful performer who integrated rock elements into his music, Brooks had topped the charts in both the rock and country categories.

But apparently alternative rock was too big a departure for his fans to tolerate. Although the album, *Garth Brooks in . . . The Life of Chris Gaines*, made it to number two on the pop album chart, and one of the singles, "Lost in You," was a top five hit, overall sales of the album were unspectacular.

Many said that Garth's fan base rejected the effort because they felt if they supported the Gaines project, they would lose the "real" Garth Brooks. Again, I'm not kidding, people were that angry and worried. Although he never once said he was giving up country, fans publicly speculated about why Garth would "do this to them."

I guess it's not just a fear of not getting your way that flatlines our thinking. Apparently the fear of losing your favorite country music singer is such a scary concept that it prompts grown people to go temporarily insane.

As someone who specializes in noncategorical thinking, I remember reading a newspaper article about the Garth Brooks–Chris Gaines quagmire and feeling the overwhelming urge to call Garth up myself and shout into the phone, "You don't have to pick, you don't have to pick! Don't let them do this to you, you can be country and alternative rock as the same time. You can wear the big hat and the goofy little goatee together, and I'll buy your stuff no matter what you're creating. Go, Garth. Go."

But alas, I don't know Garth, and my behind-the-scenes cheering wasn't enough to overcome his fans' need to keep him contained. After an initial buzz, the album sales fizzled, as the fans told Garth loud and clear, *you* might not think you have to choose categories, but we've chosen for you, so get back where you belong, big fella.

I'm probably overly sensitive to the perils of false choices and how stifling they can be, because I've spent much of my own life struggling with that very issue. Coaches, publicists, speakers' bureaus, and other experts have continually advised me that I needed to pick a lane and stay there. *Are you a business expert or self-help author? Are you a humor columnist or a spiritual writer? Do you write about relationships or pop culture? Are you a comedic speaker or an inspirational one?*

I might not have the fan base of Garth Brooks, but my inability to categorize my work has certainly caused me, and others, all kinds of confusion, and sometimes even anger.

Like the newspaper that used to run my column in the Faith and Values section and didn't appreciate it when my "Libido Thieves Ransack Suburbs" column ran alongside a commentary from a Baptist preacher. Or the HR director who hired me to train sales reps, and then found out that I had given an impromptu after-class (requested!) session advising the men how they could use the same sales techniques to woo women. Or the church that invited me to speak and was aghast when I suggested that they might have more in common with Muslims than they thought.

All I can say is, I'm sorry. I know you were all just trying to do your jobs and serve people what they expect from you. But I guess I'm just a crossover humanitarian at heart. I see the common patterns in all these areas, and it feels silly to focus on just one thing.

In terms of picking a lane for myself, as best I can describe it, I'm an expert in the way people think and how our thoughts can serve us or sabotage us. I'm fascinated by all the counterproductive ways that we keep ourselves from getting what we really want. It shows up in business, relationships, parenting, politics, and religion. And sometimes the only way I can make sense of the human condition is by helping people laugh about it.

Does that count as a lane?

My un-categorizedness doesn't present as many problems for me as it used to. But my own struggles with trying to figure out where I belong have made me acutely aware of how often we limit ourselves by trying to shortcut life and slotting people and ideas into a narrow number of categories. We then force ourselves to make choices around the categories that we, ourselves, created; we miss all kinds of opportunities. Specialization can be a good thing, when it helps us add to the big picture. I certainly wouldn't want a cancer surgeon who just dabbles around in this and that. But when our either/or instincts prompt us to narrow our thinking, it's more stifling than enhancing. We might not mean to limit ourselves, but in many cases we're either too secure in what we know or too afraid of the unknown to create anything different. Because many people are often comfortable with narrow-thinking, they often reinforce these simplistic models.

One of the reasons Jefferson and Adams were able to assimilate a nation around a new form of government, yet Garth Brooks couldn't even get his fans to embrace a new form of music, wasn't just because of the message they produced. It was the mind-set of the audiences they were playing to.

When Adams and Jefferson presented the Declaration of Independence to the Continental Congress, people were looking for answers. When Garth Brooks came out with a new sound, his fans were happy with what they already knew, so they felt no need to change.

That's one of the odd paradoxes of fear. When we're moderately afraid, we cling to what we know. But if things get really awful, and we're totally terrified, we become more willing to consider other options. It often takes a total breakdown of the system for us to step back and consider a new path. Which is why:

▸ A once-unknown one-term senator named Barack Obama was able to beat established politicians in his bid for the White House.

▸ Couples who experience a total marriage meltdown can come out stronger after they let go of their preconceived scripts of how marriage is "supposed" to work.

▸ People who experience a career crisis often find themselves on a different, more fulfilling path.

Sometimes it takes a whack over the head or a big problem for us to consider doing things in a different way. It often takes being at our lowest point for us to look beyond the obvious choices and consider new options.

Jefferson and Adams beautifully demonstrated that while assimilating conflicting ideals isn't easy, it's worth the effort. It requires that you look beyond the existing models and sometimes you have to think bigger than the people who came before you. Had our forefathers settled for the limited thinking of the past, we wouldn't have the freedoms that we do. Garth Brooks might be singing for the Queen and have no choices at all about his lyrics, and I might never have been faced with the Queen of Consumer Products quandary that prompted me to rethink what I really wanted out of life.

But sometimes it's hard to recognize a new opportunity to assimilate truths, because the person on the other side of the Triangle is more annoying than eloquent.

Are You My Thomas Jefferson?

There's nothing like a big fat fight to make you wonder why you ever hired, married, or even became friends with someone. Like the coworker who can't see the big picture or the spouse who coddles the kids when they really need a kick in the pants, or the friend who takes everything so literally that she drives you insane.

You find yourself wondering, "What are they thinking?" and if you're like me, your mind spins through the millions of examples where their wrongheaded ways have caused you problems. Time and time again, you try to co-create with them, but they just don't get it. You try to talk about feelings, they respond with facts. You believe that parents should nurture creativity in their kids; they think parenting is about instilling discipline so kids can learn to be self-reliant. You enjoy talking about the big goals; they want to know what's on the list for tomorrow morning. You believe in flexibility, they think rules make things work better.

Can you guess where I'm going with this?

The concept of opposites bringing out the best in each other is easy to understand; however, the process is anything but smooth. Some of the most productive and the most frustrating experiences of my entire life have been working alongside people who didn't think or act like me.

The most obvious example is, of course, marriage, where differences in personality and styles cause couples to bicker about everything from bill paying, to child rearing, to how to spend leisure time.

We instinctively know that creating a family (or a company or a country for that matter) is too big a challenge to base the entire thing on one set of ideas and approaches. So we tend to be attracted to people who can shore up the areas where we're weak. We're usually pleasantly aware of this when we're dating, but as any divorce lawyer will tell you, a few years of grating up against someone else's "strengths" can cause people to throw dishes at one another.

But the same thing happens in other arenas.

An exacting CEO realizes that he needs to hire more creatives because the company is filled with left-brain factoid types. Yet the first time the new art director goes on a conceptual tangent in the middle of the budget meeting, the boss wants to throw a chair at him.

The cheerleading, save-the-world church president may understand that if you can't keep the bathrooms working you might as well close the doors. However, when the fiduciary policeman on the finance committee tells her they can't afford to buy fifty new chairs because the plumbing needs an overhaul, she's likely to accuse him of not being on board with the growth plan.

The big picture VP knows that the best customer service reps connect with each customer's individual situation, yet if one of the reps suggests that the conclusions she's drawing from her global data might not apply to the guy in Tupelo, the VP is going to wonder why these frontline people can't ever see the larger vision.

We know what we need, we just don't enjoy being reminded of it. In yet another silly quagmire of the human condition, we're of the most service to the Universe when we're helping each other with the skills, ideas, and information that we lack. But the act of providing that perspective often brings out the worst in everyone.

I know this one from personal experience. I'm at my professional best when I'm helping a group of hard-charging type As learn to pause and consider the needs of the other person (so that it doesn't come back to bite them after the fact). Or when I'm teaching a bunch of put-themselves-last-on-their-own-list caregivers that they deserve to claim a space for their own needs (so they don't wind up resentful and angry).

However, I'm at my personal worst when I blow my stack at my husband because he doesn't think or act like me. In a calm moment, we may be united on the ultimate goal of raising a happy family. When I'm stressed and tired, I often feel like I'm the only one who knows how to get there, and I find myself angry with anyone who doesn't want to take the same path that I do.

Male Versus Female:
A Dichotomy Worth Mastering

It is not without coincidence that as men and women mature we often begin to acquire the traditional traits of the opposite sex. Men frequently become more nurturing, and women often become more forceful. These may be stereotypical traits, but there are numerous examples of former hard-charging, single-agenda men who become nurturing granddads, and loving, caregiving women who became kick-ass leaders after their kids are grown. Neither sex gives up their early skills and traits; they simply add to them as they age.

Much of this has to do with hormones. As a man's testosterone wanes his soft side often emerges, and as a woman's estrogen diminishes her testosterone gains more power over her thoughts.

The fact that this occurs naturally illustrates the point. When we're young and naive in our thinking, we often believe that we must be one thing or the other. As we mature, we gain more wisdom. Men often realize that caregiving is not in conflict with achieving their goals, and women frequently come to a place where they understand that pursuing their own dreams needn't conflict with nurturing the dreams of others.

Is it God granting us the grace of maturity? Maybe it's all part of Mother Nature's grand design to put us into service in one capacity early in life, and then redirect our impulses to other arenas as we get older, so that our skills and talents can be spread around for the betterment of the species. Perhaps it's because as we age we are all meant to become leaders, and good leaders combine both nurturing and strength. Or maybe it's just a big hormonal mess, and adopting the traits of the other side as we get older is the only thing that keeps us from killing each other in a long-term marriage.

Who knows, but it's also worth noting that our collective view of such matters has changed quite dramatically over time, particularly in the last few years. Younger men and women, while often conflicted about these issues, do not seem to feel nearly the same compulsion to make definitive, limiting choices that their parents once did. A social dynamic that beautifully illustrates Darwin's theory of evolution, the fittest do survive and the fittest are those who best adapt to their environment and whose behaviors improve the development of future generations.

The most successful people—with success defined as loving what they do, loving who they do it with, and loving their whole life—are usually those who combine the traditional masculine and feminine traits.

Again, we don't have to choose, we can do—and be—both.

False Choices of Substance and Style

Boxing ourselves into false choices limits us in every aspect of our lives. Battles over what people assume to be either/or choices cause conflict in our personal lives; they keep us from innovating in our work and dumb down our politics.

False choices create turf wars in business when people assume that one function has to take precedence over another in organizational decisions. They create spiritual problems when people believe that one religious path is more worthy than another. They create problems in communities when people polarize around issues, reactively assuming that there's not enough time, space, or money to accomplish everyone's goals.

But it's not just false choices about budgets, organizational strategy, or religious rituals that limit us. Sometimes we box ourselves into false choices about style and emotions, believing that there is only one way to manage, organize, or even parent.

Parenting expert Amy McCready says that one of the biggest issues parents in her workshops struggle with is the belief that they have to choose between authoritative and permissive parenting. Most parents tend to gravitate toward one or the other, either the style they were raised with, or what suits their personality type; or in some cases, they're trying to do the opposite of their own parents.

Most of the parents at McCready's seminars are there because the way they're doing it isn't working, yet they're still reluctant to give it up. They say things like, "I'm not going to be one of those parents who just lets their kids run wild, it's my job to control them." Or "I was raised by parents who made their kids live in fear, but I want my kids to grow up feeling accepted and loved."

But the choice between authoritative and permissive parenting is a false choice. And it's interesting that when people talk about the subject they frequently describe their style in terms of what they don't want to be. Reactive "I'm not going to do it this way so I have to do it that way" type of thinking is frequently what causes us to fall into false choices.

In the case of parenting, the real duality parents need to assimilate is structure and freedom.

McCready says, "When we feel like things are out of control, our natural inclination is to try to clamp down." This creates negative outcomes as the child inevitably resists, or worse, loses their spirit and becomes passive and broken. However, she says, "If you have no limits and take an 'I just want to be your friend and I just want you to love me' approach, that, too, has negative outcomes." As anyone who has ever had to live with a two-year-old that didn't have a regular nap schedule can attest.

However, McCready says that once parents understand that they can provide structure while at the same time giving the child lots of freedom within that structure, it's like a lightbulb goes off. Parents are frequently moved to tears when they realize they can love their child and be the boss at the same time.

It's no coincidence that McCready is a highly successful parenting expert. She spent fifteen years as a corporate executive mastering the duality of structure and freedom with several hundred people on a national team.

The false choices that we create in the parenting realm are no different than the false choices we create at work or in other situations. We look at the existing models and try to choose the one we think will work best. Or we react to what we don't want and assume that the only choice is to gravitate to the other side.

What is really required is some thoughtful thinking about what we're actually trying to accomplish.

▶ Is it an organization with firm fiscal controls *And* the financial flexibility to pursue new opportunities?

► Is it a country where people are free to create their own success *And* that has regulations that prevent people from taking advantage of others?

► Is it raising future citizens who know how to comply with the law *And* who also have a strong sense of their own self-worth?

When we clarify our desired outcomes we can create new paths for all areas of our lives—lives that need not be limited by choices of the past, but that can be reinvented as we find new ways.

The Third Path: A Call to Intellectual Maturity

When we lose sight of what we're actually trying to achieve, our thinking flatlines, and we assume that the only way to achieve our goal is to choose between option A or option B. But if we can open our hearts and ask someone who holds a different perspective for help in co-creating, we will create new choices. If we can tolerate the ambiguity of holding seemingly conflicting perspectives in our mind at the same time, there's no limit to what we can do.

We don't have to choose between the two existing paths; we can create a third path.

We can be like the superstar reps, and see the forest *And* the trees.

We can assimilate the big picture with the day-to-day by

holding a larger mission in our hearts, while at the same time lovingly attending to the details of the mundane. We can add meaning to our tasks by continually grounding ourselves in a larger vision, a vision that extends beyond our own self-interest to connect us with others and put us into service for the greater good.

We can be like Stockdale, assimilating facts *And* faith.

We can have the courage to face up to the reality of our situation, yet never give in to hopelessness and despair. We can refuse to succumb to the delusions of false optimism, while at the same time holding on to our faith that things will eventually work out OK. We can let go of our need to control everything, because we know that if we show up with love and discipline, with our minds ready to tackle the tasks at hand, we will prevail in whatever we endeavor.

We can be like great parents who create environments of discipline *And* creativity.

We can be like Jefferson and Adams, embracing freedom *And* responsibility.

We can step into responsibility by creating a system that affords our fellow humans the freedom to follow their own best impulses. We can create a culture of both personal and collective responsibility by allowing people the freedom to better their own lives as well as the lives of others.

We can hold people accountable without holding them in contempt. We can condemn the actions of ego without condemning the value of souls. We can protect the interests of the many while understanding that circumstances often conspire to bring out the worst in a few. We can extend compassion for the collective spirit as we create a just world for each and every person in it.

We can be like Albert Einstein, drawing wisdom from science *And* religion.

We can aggressively pursue new discoveries secure in the knowledge that new information will only deepen our understanding of timeless spiritual truths. We can use our intellect in the service of our souls by seeking to better comprehend the mysteries of the world that has been bestowed upon us. We can honor the divinity of nature by unraveling the intricacies of it.

And yes, we can even talk and have sex.

But we will not be able to combine any of these high-level conceptual truths if we are too intellectually immature to look beyond the simple choices currently being presented. Choices that our minds may prefer, because they are comfortable and easy to understand, but choices that are nonetheless false, and limit our potential over the long haul.

It is an immaturity of thought and spirit that causes us to create false choices. Yet when we are able to rise above this tendency, we not only create more fulfilling lives for ourselves, we are also more likely to create new paradigms that will benefit others.

The Triangle of Truth is a call to maturity—intellectual, emotional, and spiritual maturity—because it is a call for us to see beyond the presenting options. It takes strength of character to elevate your mind to a conceptual level in the face of existing choices that are bound by the limits of literal thinking. And it is particularly challenging to think conceptually when the pace of our lives pushes us toward constantly navigating the all too real logistics of getting through each day.

Couple that with our natural predisposition for certain truths and it is no wonder that we are more likely to just choose one of the presenting paths rather than pause to consider creating a new way. But a predisposition toward one side or the other needn't limit us to that choice. If anything, a preference for one path should prompt us to pay more careful attention to the people who are suggesting another.

Assimilating perspectives is not easy, and the path is not often obvious at first glance. That doesn't mean we can't do it. If Jefferson and Adams could find a way to work together, so can we.

You don't have to see both sides of the Triangle, you just have to be open to working with someone who cares deeply about the side you're inclined to ignore.

Thomas Jefferson and John Adams came together in a moment of brilliance. Together they helped birth a nation, and through their disagreements, they continued to make it a better one. They didn't always appreciate each other, but their differences forced them both to be better.

It might be easier to work or stay married to people who agree with us on everything. But often, the people who disagree with us are helping us even more. Jefferson and Adams didn't settle for the convenience of false choices, because they knew that their country deserved the best.

We still do. Not just as a nation, but as individuals, families, companies, and communities. The process of co-creating is messy, argumentative, and sometimes even painful, but that doesn't mean we should abandon it.

John Adams always said that he would outlive Thomas Jefferson. He was right, but only by a few hours. However, when he passed away on the afternoon of that July 4, he thought Jefferson was still alive.

Popular history says that John Adams's last words were "Jefferson survives." But his niece Louisa Smith, who was with him when he died, said that the last words he distinctly spoke were "Thomas Jefferson," the rest of his softly whispered sentence too incoherent to understand. Was his ego terrified of what might happen if he left the earth with Jefferson still in it?

Or was his soul eager to greet his partner and frequent nemesis on the other side?

Perhaps both. Perhaps, in the space between his last breath and his passing, John Adams saw the beauty of it all. He saw how the Universe had sent two stubborn idealists to the time and place the world needed them most. How their ideals and their love for their cause had conspired to create something amazing at a time when much of the world didn't even believe it possible. And perhaps he also saw how he had become a better person as a result of it.

If there is an afterlife, I imagine Mr. Jefferson and Mr. Adams in their breeches and wigs, greeting each other with a hearty handshake, saying, "Well done, partner. Well done."

The path to greatness is forged by people who have the courage to assimilate big picture truths. So the next time you find yourself in a situation where it seems like you have to choose between two important ideals, or you're arguing with someone about one idea versus another, pause and ask yourself, Do we really have to decide? Is this all we are capable of being? Or is there another way?

And if you're feeling frustrated with the people around you, you might want to consider the possibility that perhaps the Universe has sent you a John Adams.

Discern Intent

Discovering the Real Truth Behind
Imperfect Solutions

All general judgments are loose and imperfect.
—Michel de Montaigne, French philosopher
and writer (1533–1592)

As the two groups stood to address the crowd it was obvious they were at a total impasse. They even took positions on opposite sides of the stage, as if to further illustrate their differences. Tempers were running high and the whole organization appeared to be on the verge of collapse.

As the spokesperson for each group made their case to the assembly, one wondered how people who had once publicly pledged to come together for the greater good had become so quickly divided.

The committee chair went first. "They have a totally different vision for the organization than we do." she said, "They don't really care about the people that we're supposed to serve."

The other side countered, "Their group has had problems for years, we just can't find a way to work with them, the only way we can fix this is to tear down the whole infrastructure and rebuild it."

"Tear it down—are you kidding? The reason it's not working is because you all keep undermining our efforts. We're supposed to be in charge of this, yet you all make decisions without even consulting us."

"We ask for your input, but you're totally unwilling to compromise, you don't see the big picture, all you care about is your one area."

As the two groups argued, you could feel the crowd splitting as well, as onlookers found themselves casting their sentiments with one group or the other.

What kind of meeting was it? A company retreat gone bad? A town hall with citizens arguing over policy? A legislative session with warring committees trying to win the public's vote?

None of the above. It was the annual meeting of a 125-member church, and the fight was between the Board of Trustees and the Religious Education Committee, both of whom felt the other group was undermining the entire organization.

Which is kind of ironic, since this particular church's core principles are to affirm and promote "the inherent worth and dignity of every person" as well as "justice, equity, and compassion in human relations." They even have a poster proclaiming it in the lobby. But when emotions are involved, sometimes it's hard to remember how you originally wanted to behave.

In the case of the bickering church members, the original intent on both sides was to create a caring community for everyone. One group, the Board of Trustees, was charged with managing the resources for the entire community, while the other group, the Religious Education Committee, was charged with creating programs for children.

Problems arose when a lack of funds forced the board to make some tough decisions that didn't sit well with the smaller group. That's when, despite it being a church setting, all hell broke loose. People who once stood side by side pledging to love and support each other through thick and thin wound up pointing fingers and asking fellow church members to choose sides.

It's a classic example of what happens when you start attributing bad intent. You create all kinds of conflict and angst. That's why when you're in a conflict, it's critical to discern the truth. The real truth, the truth behind the solutions.

Solutions are based on what someone thinks is the best way to solve a problem. It's just one person or group's idea about how to tackle whatever issue they're confronting. Intent is another thing altogether. You might not like their solution, and it may be based on limited information or a narrow perspective. But chances are they didn't come up with it with the sole intention of ruining you, or the project, or the company, or the country.

However, if you can dig behind their solution, to uncover their intent, you'll often discover a truth that you might agree with.

For example, when the accountants come up with a plan requiring three levels of sign-offs for all purchases over two dollars, their truth is probably not, "We're blanketing the company with needless paperwork because we want productivity to come to a screeching halt." That may be your perception of their solution. Their actual truth is probably something more along the lines of, "We want good financial controls so that we don't waste money."

The latter is something very few people would argue with. How you create a system that supports that truth is something you can work out together. But until you discern their real truth, you're probably just going to continue fighting.

The same thing holds true in personal situations. A parent tells her teenager, "You can't go to this party because there won't be any adults there." The teen hears, "You don't trust me, and you want to keep me chained to the front porch." The parent's real truth is more likely, "I love you and I'm doing my best to keep you safe." The teen's truth is probably along the lines of, "I'm an adult in training, and I need to be able control my own life."

However, getting the real truth on the table can be a challenge, because we're often so locked into our solutions that we feel as though they are the truth.

One of our consulting partners, Bill Albert, describes a meeting in which the VP of HR for a hospital chain almost walked out the door when her truth felt violated. When asked about how the hospital looked at paying versus nonpaying patients, she said, "If we even talk about how some patients are paid and some are not it would imply that some patients are better than others. As far as I'm concerned this meeting is finished, I can't go back to my people and tell them that some patients have a higher priority."

Whereupon the finance person said, "It costs me two million a day to keep this facility open. Everyone deserves great care, and we're not saying that we shouldn't care for people who can't pay, but we need to make money so we can keep the doors open."

The care versus finance dichotomy is an issue we encounter every day in our training and consulting work. Bill sums it up well when he says, "At the end of the day both people want their hospital or medical center to be first rate, but they have polar opposite approaches to looking at the business."

The compassion versus fiscal prudence quagmire is something that's easy for us to understand, because it plays out in so many situations. On a heart level very few of us would let another human being suffer just because they didn't have money. Yet we can all also relate to the very real challenge of trying to make ends meet when there's not enough cash coming in the door.

It's not an easily solvable problem, in any organization, but you can't make much progress if the stakeholders can't even bear to be in the same room together. That's why our Triangle of Truth training programs are designed to bring the various factions to the table. One of the techniques we use is putting people into the role of the other person, and asking them to make decisions based on what that person or group is responsible for. It's shocking how quickly people uncover another department's core truths when they're suddenly responsible for their job function.

Digging for the real truths behind the solutions enables people to get past their animosity and work on creating different alternatives that are built on the truth of both sides. But it's hard to discover truths when you're attributing bad intent to the other party. And you can't create new solutions if you stay stuck on judging the current imperfect ones.

Judgment Versus Discernment

One of our biggest obstacles to creating new paradigms is that we judge what is, without even considering what can be. In business, in government, in families, and in relationships, we are often so focused on rejecting the imperfect ideas of others, that we limit our ability to create.

Just as self-absorbed fear keeps us from connecting with those who have a different agenda, fear-based judgments about less than perfect solutions block us from manifesting anything different. When we're afraid that someone's solution is in conflict with our own, we judge them as wrong. We attribute bad intent, and we're unable to see any inherent truths behind the less than perfect solution they're suggesting. When our energy is directed toward proving our own judgments right, we stay stuck arguing about who's right and who's wrong. If we can move beyond judgment into true discernment, we will likely often uncover truths that can serve as a basis for rising above existing arguments.

Words can be tricky. They only mean what we think they mean, and if I mean one thing and you think I mean another, we're not in sync.

The word *judgment* gets both a good and a bad rap. On the one hand, many believe that judgment is a bad thing. Who are we to judge the thoughts and deeds of another? It's not up to us to play God and decide such matters. However, we want leaders to exercise good judgment. We teach our children to use their judgment. And we certainly want a society that is fair and just.

Yet very few of us wish to be judged ourselves, and we commonly criticize other people for being too judgmental. Unless of course they're actual robe-wearing judges, in which case we often judge them for being bad judges. It's OK for them to judge, unless we judge them to be bad at it.

We don't want to sit in judgment of others, yet you can't make good hiring decisions without judging who's going to work hard versus who's going to be a drain on your payroll. How can you decide who's best suited for your team if you don't judge them on their skills and work habits? How are your kids supposed to choose a college, or you supposed to choose a candidate without judging? And what in the world will happen to *American Idol* if we as a society give up judging?

In his bestselling book *Blink*, author Malcolm Gladwell analyzes the snap judgments that we make about others, and he discovers that despite being told that we shouldn't judge on first impressions, our initial assessments are frequently quite accurate. In the blink of an eye our subconscious mind assimilates data that we didn't even know we had and reaches uncannily correct conclusions about people and situations.

However, and this is a very important point, Gladwell also reveals how our own prejudices can affect our judgment, and why the people who make the best instantaneous assessments are those who are truly experts in their fields and have amassed huge amounts of information in their brains.

Tennis pros with years of experience coaching can quickly spot which players are most likely to double-fault. And art experts who have spent thousands of hours cataloguing great works can tell instantly if a statue is a fake.

If I were to try to pick out the best tennis players or determine the age of a statue, I would probably make snap judgments based on what the players looked like, or how crumbly the statue was, and I would likely be wrong. Because I know very little about either of those areas.

Which is why judgment is problematic.

When we judge the solutions being presented by others, we view them through our own prejudice and biases, and we often reach conclusions based on our own very limited information.

What if instead of constantly judging, we reframed our thinking and focused on discernment instead?

*   *   *

Webster's defines *judgment* as, "a formal utterance of an authoritative opinion" and "an opinion so pronounced." However, *discernment* is defined as "the quality of being able to grasp and comprehend what is obscure," and the "power to see what is not evident to the average mind."

It can happen in the blink of an eye, as when your intuition tells you that the guy approaching you in the parking garage is bad news, without you even realizing that your subconscious mind has already processed details about his facial expressions, his walk, and the fact that his eyes keep darting from side to side. Or it can take longer, like during a two-hour interview process or in years of studying salespeople and trying to figure out what makes them tick.

Discernment is the ability to use both your conscious mind *And* your subconscious to ferret out the truth. The difference between discernment and judgment is the difference between trying to truly understand something (discernment) and applying your own emotional baggage to it, which is the judgment.

Yes, the guy in the parking lot may be out to harm you, but you have no idea how or why he ended up being a criminal, and you just need to get away. And yes, the person who showed up unprepared and couldn't string two words together might not be the best candidate to become your new assistant or our next president, but that doesn't mean they're morally bankrupt as a human being.

Our challenge in assimilating agendas with people with whom we differ is to discern their truths, without judging their solutions. We need to discern their true intention, without casting judgment on their ideas.

Survival Techniques of the Lizard

Fear and judgment go hand in hand. Circling back to the reptilian brain, up until a few generations ago, it was critically important to make snap judgments. We needed to decide whether someone was friend or foe, whether the berries were yummy or poisonous, and whether that big animal was slow enough and stupid enough for us to capture it, or whether it was fast enough and smart enough to capture us. Judging incorrectly meant the difference between life and death, and it was best to err on the side of fear and caution.

If you decided that someone is a potential foe, and they really wanted to be friends, you might stay lonely, but at least you'd be alive. However, if you judged them to be a potential new buddy, and they turned out to be otherwise, you could find yourself roasting in a fire pit, while their family drools over the yummy entree mom or dad brought home.

However, unless you're a soldier in combat or braving the snakes in the Amazon, very few of the decisions we make now are life-and-death matters that must be decided within the next two seconds.

It's challenging to avoid making judgments in even calm, low-risk situations. It's particularly difficult when someone is presenting a solution that we believe in our hearts is just plain wrong.

Studies show that when you hear something that fits with what you already know, the pleasure center of your brain lights up. However, if you hear something that doesn't fit with what you believe, your pain center lights up. It's all in our subconscious, but it explains why we have the reactions we do, and why we get so emotional when a loved one, neighbor, politician, or even a stranger says something we disagree with. For example, if someone tells you that "all children need a good whippin' to keep them in line," you're likely to judge them as a less than enlightened parent. However, there's very little likelihood that you will be able to convince them that corporal punishment is wrong if you're sitting in judgment about their decision to enact it.

Many people who believe in spanking their children claim they do so because they want to raise children who can follow the rules required to function in society. If you can discern some inherent truth behind their actions, you might be able to suggest alternative ways to get there.

In this case, their truth may be that undisciplined children make themselves and everyone else miserable (true) or that the best place to learn self-discipline is from your parents (also true). This in no way conflicts with an important truth of those who typically oppose physical discipline, which is that children learn to respect others by the way their parents respect them.

> **When we make judgments about someone's suggested solutions, we lose the ability to influence their thinking.**

Uncovering each other's core truths opens up a plane of agreement upon which we can build. It's the base of the Triangle so to speak. Truths tend to be conceptual, while solutions are more literal. When people feel that their truths have been heard and understood, they're more likely to be flexible about creating alternative paths.

However, when we make judgments about someone's suggested solutions, we lose the ability to influence their thinking. For example:

- ▸ If you believe the people who created the budget are operating from a place of corruption and greed, it's highly unlikely that you're going to be able to convince them to give your group more money.

- ▸ If you think that your spouse is operating on a plane of selfishness, it's improbable that you're going to be able to persuade them to take over more of the household chores.

- ▸ If you're convinced that your in-laws are intent on making your life miserable, it's going to be challenging for you to co-create a plan for a joint summer vacation.

You have little moral authority over people whom you disdain. However, if we can let go of our emotional judgments and try to discern the intent behind someone's actions or ideas, we will get one step closer to the truth.

Discerning Their Truth, Even When You're Annoyed

Discerning the truths behind someone's solutions is a challenge, because it requires us to look for potential good intent behind actions that we don't like. This is hardly our typical default response to conflict and disagreement.

If someone cuts you off midsentence during an important meeting, and proceeds to tell the whole group why your idea is wrong, and that everyone should do what he suggests instead, it's going to be quite challenging for you to pause, take a breath, and say with true sincerity, "Oh really, please tell us more about your idea, so that I can discern all the great truths you are so graciously sharing Mr. Interrupter. Because I know that you want the best for our group as much as I do and I'm sure there's a way that all our ideas can come together and create a whole that is bigger than any of us could create alone. That's why I'm so appreciative of you cutting me off in the middle of my presentation, because had everyone just gone along with my plan, as they were clearly about to do before you so helpfully interrupted, we might have missed your valuable input. So thank you, Mr. Single Agenda, for making me and, quite frankly, this whole group better. You're just a regular Thomas Jefferson, aren't you, big fella?"

It might not be your natural inclination to pause and listen when you've been challenged. But the fake-it-till-you-make-it, practice-it-before-you-actually-feel-it approach works here as well. If we can resist judgment and discipline our minds to seek the real truth even 5 percent of the time, or for even five minutes in any given argument, things will change.

Trying to discern the truth often means that you have to take a leadership role in the conversation. This means recasting arguments away from a solution debate and refocusing the dialogue on the motivations behind them. They may be hell-bent on a particular solution, but if you can get to the root of how they came up with it, you may be able to discern a truth that you can support.

The best way to do that is with questions, but you have to be very intentional. This is a situation where tone and body language are everything.

If you're in the middle of a conflict, and you bark out, "Why do you think *that* is the best way to solve this problem?" with an unspoken "You stupid moron, why would you ever think *that* would work?" chances are you're not going to uncover a higher truth. More than likely you're just going to descend even further into an either/or fight.

If you ask the same question, yet preface it with a deep breath, a pause, and a loving thought in your mind, it's going to come out sounding differently. You don't even have to hold loving thoughts about the person; you can hold a loving thought about anything. It can be the organization you're arguing about, or the people you're trying to serve, or the group you're trying to support. You can even think about your kids or chocolate, anything that activates the loving, caring spot in your brain.

If you can introduce your question by saying, "Hmm, I never thought about doing that, you're obviously an intelligent person, I'm eager to know more, can you tell me why you think that's the best way to solve this problem?" you're more likely to move out of conflict into discussion. You may find yourself having to do it several times before it starts to work, but well-intended questions are one of the best ways to recast go-nowhere arguments.

> **Well-intended questions are one of the best ways to recast go-nowhere arguments.**

But it's important to remember, when you're trying to discern the truth behind something you disagree with, that the first thing you need to do is calm yourself down. Only then can you can turn your attention to the other party with calm, nonjudgmental questions.

Here's how a reframe might have worked in the bickering church scenario that opened this chapter. What might have happened if, in the middle of the big public fight, or ideally earlier, when the disagreements first started, the head of one group had said to the other, "I love this community so much, and I'm so committed to these people. I know you love these people, too, and that we're all trying to do our best in a challenging situation. Can you please help me understand how you all came to these decisions?"

Something tells me they wouldn't have been ready to assault each other from either side of the pulpit.

First Truth Versus Second Truth Battles

One of the reasons we so frequently find ourselves at odds with people who claim to care about the same things we do is that we have different primary motivations and functions.

For example, in the battle between care and finance, the people on the care side want to be part of a fiscally responsible organization, and the people on the finance side want to provide care. But what is one person's primary function and motivation, their first truth if you will, is often a secondary truth to the other person. The finance people want great care for everyone, but their primary job is to make sure the place doesn't go broke.

When someone else's solution threatens your first truth, it often doesn't matter if what they're suggesting supports your secondary truth; all you can see is that your first truth is at risk, and so you react accordingly.

Politics is an arena where the "cling to the first truth, abandon the second truth" dynamic plays out all the time (especially in the fiscal prudence versus social responsibility battle).

Not many people would want to live in a country that throws away money, nor would they want to live in one that has no compassion for its citizens. Yet to hear some people talk you would think one side was suggesting that the government pass out dollar bills on street corners so that the populist can roll them into joints and smoke them. The other side has practically been accused of taking money out of the mouths of starving babies in order to create systems that penalize the poor.

When we accuse well-intended people of harboring ill intent simply because their less than robust solutions violate one of our own truths, they're more likely to defend them than they are to expand them.

One of the more emotional first truth versus secondary truth battles many of us experience is in in-law situations. The family of origin (the parents) wants to create a happy family. They also want their children to create their own successful families, but the way they (the original parents) typically define themselves is in terms of their own family. How often they get together, how close they are, how much they all enjoy doing the same things, and how they all love to uphold the traditions, activities, and ideas that were established when their kids were young. This is their first truth.

Enter the interlopers, the outside spouses, who usually start off sincerely wanting to have a good relationship with their in-laws, and would never begrudge their spouse a close relationship with their parents (in theory). Yet the new spouse's primary agenda is to create their own happy family. Should they feel that their ability to do this is being threatened by their spouse's parents they will respond accordingly.

It would be nice if everyone could have both, if the older parents could have their happy family and sleep secure knowing that their children were also creating happy families in their own right. And it would help enormously if the new younger family could create their own satisfying rituals and traditions while also enjoying the traditions of the family of origin.

But if either party finds themselves in a situation where their first truth feels threatened, they will forget about their second truth and direct all of their energy toward defending their number one goal.

If the parents suggest spending the holidays with all their collective children and their spouses and their kids crammed into their split-level ranch, and the younger family would rather spend their holiday creating a bonding ritual for their own little nuclear family, both sides will accuse the other of not caring.

> **When someone else's solution threatens a person's first truth, their instinct is to abandon what may have once been their secondary agenda.**

When someone else's solution threatens a person's first truth, the latter's instinct is to abandon what may have once been their secondary agenda. If Person A's solution violates Person B's truth, all bets are off. Each side will correctly ascertain that the other side doesn't give a fig about their all-important truth. And they will be right, because in the heat of the moment, people don't care about the second truth; they only care about the first one.

Abandoning the second truth in order to defend the first truth happens to us in a multitude of situations. The talking-versus-sex debate is a classic first-truth-versus-second-truth conflict. Very few men or women would want a sexless marriage or a talkless one. Yet if your primary need is at risk, you often forget that you also enjoy having your secondary needs met. People will create all kinds of drama if their partner proposes a solution that doesn't support their first truth.

Sadly, sometimes all it takes is an imperfect solution for us to start attributing bad intent.

Imperfect Solutions:
Turf Wars

Attributing bad intent is why so many organizations experience turf wars. They occur in business, philanthropy, and even families. Each group has a different function, yet instead of assimilating with each other, they frequently find themselves bickering, because each group believes that the other group doesn't get it, and even worse, they suspect them of treachery toward the organization, which is particularly painful for people who care about the bigger picture.

One of the common turf wars in business is IT versus operations. The IT group rolls out a new software package, glitches occur, and then the finger pointing begins.

Operations says, "Those IT guys don't really care about our company and our customers. They just want to get credit for the cool factor, and move onto the next project. They don't understand the implications of their actions."

The people in IT say, "We're trying to provide these people with state-of-the art programs and all they do is complain. They don't even care how much work went into this. One little thing goes wrong, and they declare the sky is falling."

Both groups are quick to suggest that the other guys don't care. All mistakes and problems are seen through the filter of "If you really cared about this company the way I do you wouldn't act like this."

From an outside perspective, it's easy to see that both groups are just trying to do their jobs. But to the people locked inside the conflict, the other side is often judged as downright evil. Getting emotional and assuming ill-intent might seem silly in a business setting, but it happens quite often. One of the most popular articles on our website is "Top 10 Turf Wars and How to Solve Them." Yet we also do the same thing in our personal lives. Our spouse suggests a weekend plan we don't like, and we accuse them of not caring about our needs. Our neighbor wants to change the community bylaws in a way that will negatively impact us, and we judge them as self-serving.

It's difficult to see good intent and discern someone's truths when their solutions are negatively affecting us. Yet those are the exact situations where we need to do it most.

In the case of the IT versus operations war, it's obvious that they need to be working together on behalf of the bigger picture, but it's hard to assimilate truths if you think the other side is out to do you wrong.

That's why when you're stuck in a conflict trying to discern the other side's actual intent is one of the best first steps in getting the real truths on the table.

What might happen if instead of accusing the IT guys of not caring, one of the Ops people had gone to the head of IT and said, "It must be frustrating to have people complain so much, what are your hopes for your next launch?" That statement validates their frustrations and invites them to share their intent, which is probably something that none of the complainers ever did before.

Discerning intent and uncovering the other side's core truths is what enables you to use the Triangle of Truth in potentially volatile and emotional situations. I've found that if you're willing to withhold judgment, sometimes the very people you thought would never change are the ones who most surprise you.

Discerning Intent in Emotionally Charged Debates

Parenting is one of the most emotionally charged subjects there is. People care immensely about it, and very few people think anyone else does it right. Discipline is a particular hot button. Since I've already brought up the subject of corporal punishment, let's see how discerning intent might be helpful in a discussion about spanking.

A generation ago, spanking was considered the norm. Today there's an ever-growing group of parents and childcare experts who believe it's wrong. However, there are also many people who believe that physical discipline is one of the best ways to get a child's attention.

I was spanked as a child by my own well-intentioned parents, and while I seem to have recovered, I'm now in the nonspanking camp myself.

I can stand on a mountaintop and preach the ills of spanking until I'm blue in the face. I can accuse people of giving into their own anger. I can tell them when you use violence on a child, you teach them to use violence on others. But I will have little chance of changing anyone's mind with that sort of one-way preaching.

However, if I can put aside my judgments about someone's choice of a discipline solution and discern what their real intent is for their children, it's more likely that I will find a truth I can support. By showing them that I understand and am in agreement with their truth, which is likely that they love their children and want them to turn out well, I am in a much better position to influence their thinking.

Is it hard? You better believe it is. It takes patience, and intellectual fortitude, because sometimes people say and do such crazy things they make you want to scream.

But I know a certain teenage girl whose well-intended yet frequently reactive father used to hit her with a belt, who will tell you that it's worth it. Getting involved in other people's lives isn't always appropriate, but there are times when your heart calls on you to intervene. Good people can often find themselves so stressed-out that they just repeat what's been done to them. But it's only because they don't know how to create anything different. However, if you can soften your heart, withhold judgment, and show them that you're on their side, you often find yourself in a position to positively influence their thinking.

This is another one of those silly human quagmires. When people are being pushed to change, they resist with all their might, even if what they're doing is clearly not working. But when they feel supported for who they are, the motivation to change often comes from within. When you are able to discern the good intent behind their less than perfect solution, they often ask you for advice—the very same advice they would have resisted had you criticized their solution from the start.

If you're thinking, "Well, this is so stupid. I'm trying to help people yet I have to patiently work through a process of validating them and making them feel good so that I can set them up to receive information that they really should have asked for in the first place." Yep, that about sums it up, and you're right, it is stupid. But that's the way people are.

I spent two decades training people and all I can say is, the more insecure and narrow-minded they are, the more time you have to spend coddling them so that they can feel good enough about themselves to actually learn something.

Stepping into others people's problems isn't always the right thing to do. But if find yourself in a situation where you have the opportunity to influence a situation, sometimes the stakes are just too high to step away. You owe it to yourself and all the parties involved to do the best job you possibly can. Sure, it would be easier to just speak your peace and move on, but if you're willing to take the time to discern intent, people are often more open to change than you might suspect.

As cheesy as it sounds, we really are the heroes we've been waiting for. Who is going to help us break out of our either/or paradigms if not us?

The only way for us to solve our age-old arguments is for

someone to be willing to recast the conversation. And sometimes that means being willing to open our minds and talk
about some tough issues.

The Either/Or Debate That
Tops Them All

It was originally a Hopi Elder who said, "We are the ones we have
been waiting for." The prophecy is one of peace, protecting both
land and life.

It is with thoughts of peace and protecting what we hold most
dear that I address how the Triangle of Truth might be applied
to one of the most polarizing debates of our time: abortion.

If there ever was a topic where there's not much middle ground,
it's this one. Nothing symbolizes an either/or debate more than
the two warring factions on either side of an abortion picket line.
The people on both sides accuse the other of immorality, and a
total lack of compassion for human life.

All the energy is directed at proving why the other side is
wrong, wrong, wrong. There is the assumption of bad intent on
both sides, and people have even resorted to violence.

When it's distilled down, one side believes that it's morally
wrong to make a woman have a baby she doesn't want; the
people on the other side believe that it is morally wrong to have
an abortion. There's not much room in the middle.

With both sides so vehemently arguing their competing
truths, there's little energy left to create an alternative solution.

I suspect that one hundred years from now people will look

back on us as barbarians. "Can you believe that women actually had abortions? Or that they ever had babies they didn't want? Gosh, they were so primitive. They didn't know how to go into the techno vapor-lock and tap into their spiritual and physical center to create a plan for how many children they wanted to bring into the world. Boy, were they ill-informed."

It's not unintentional that I describe the future using the language of both science and spirit. I believe with all my heart that the solution is ultimately going to be rooted in the truths of both these worlds. Yet it's a solution we're not going to find when many of our best minds are still fighting about the problem.

Earlier in this book, I offered a quote about how both sides in a debate are frequently right about what they affirm and wrong in what they deny. I think it applies here. Until we acknowledge the truth on both sides of this argument, we're not going to get anywhere. All our energy will be directed toward the fighting.

I've presented this idea in public forums, to both pro-choice and pro-life groups, and the most common reactions I get are:

"If we concede that they have a point, they'll use that against us and get the laws changed faster than you can say moral outrage."

"If we give these people an inch they'll take a mile. They have no compassion. We can't put aside our position because we're right, and if we back down, they'll win."

If you're staunchly in either camp, please understand, I'm not suggesting you give up your truth—quite the contrary.

I'm suggesting that we will make more progress if we can put our own truths on pause and listen to the other side—which is extremely hard to do. When you're emotionally attached to an outcome, sometimes it's hard to imagine a different solution than the one based on the truth you hold most dear.

But perhaps both sides are right. Their solutions may be in conflict with each other, but perhaps their core truths are not. Perhaps the only real problem is that we haven't found a way to bring them together.

Their solutions may be in conflict with each other, but perhaps their core truths are not.

There are very few people on the pro-choice side who think that abortion is no big deal. Just as there aren't many people on the pro-life side who want to bring more unwanted babies into the world.

Certainly, there are extremists, and unfortunately they often appoint themselves as chief spokespersons for their side. But if you ask the average person, most people believe that finding a way to prevent abortion *And* unplanned pregnancy is a good thing.

However, what often happens is that the people who see both sides, or who at least have some compassion for the other side, are reluctant to talk about it, because it's such a controversial topic. This leaves the single-minded zealots in control of the debate, while the problem continues to go unsolved.

Abortion is an area where for most, there is no compromise. That's why it's time to stop battling over the middle ground and start seeking the higher ground.

* * *

It's not our beliefs about the two currently competing truths that are holding us back; it's our belief that they are somehow incompatible. If we can validate the core truths on both sides—no woman should have an abortion and no woman should be forced to have a baby she doesn't want—and use those truths as the foundation for a dialogue, we might open up a space for different solutions. Solutions that are based on the core truths of both sides, because ultimately, the truth is never in conflict with the truth. The truth is just that, the truth. It is only the solutions we've created around our truths that are divergent. We won't come up with new solutions until we acknowledge the possibility that they might exist.

When John F. Kennedy told America that we were going to put a man on the moon, we didn't know exactly how that was going to happen. When a leader puts the best minds in the world on a problem, they find a way to chart a new frontier.

Solving the abortion issue isn't as cool as creating rockets and space suits. But to a lot of people, it matters even more. What would happen if the president or another leader put the scientists, spiritual leaders, teen moms, and social workers all in a room and said, "In five years, I want no more abortions and no more unwanted pregnancies. Figure it out, people. Failure is not an option."

I'd send them a check, offer to facilitate the meeting, and bring in snacks while they worked.

The process of assimilating truths can be messy, uncomfortable, and sometimes painful. And the abortion issue is one of the messiest, most uncomfortable, painful issues around. We've made progress; we now have adoption, sex education, birth control, and a whole host of other options we didn't have a few decades ago. Perhaps there are other even more spiritually enlightened, scientifically grounded solutions out there just waiting for us to discover them. However, we won't find those more creative solutions until we direct our collective energies toward looking for them.

We as citizens have the power to recast this debate, in our homes and in our communities. We can move away from arguing the merits of imperfect solutions, and begin to search for a new path.

If we continue to expend all of our energy vocalizing our opposition to the other side, and accusing them of bad intent toward humankind, we'll stay stuck right where we are. But if we can decide that we want something better for everyone, perhaps we will find a new way.

Be the Hero (Somebody Has To)

The Triangle of Truth is a call to listen to our better angels, and it is a tool we can use to help other people find their better angels as well. If we truly want to change the dialogue, we are the ones who must lead the way. Yes, it's that damn hero thing again. We are the ones the world has been waiting on. We can whine and dither about how other people should be more enlightened and open-minded, or we can just start helping them get there.

If we want to recast disagreements, diffuse anger, and solve problems, we must make a conscious effort to discern the real truths behind the imperfect solutions that others are offering.

Discerning the truth doesn't mean that you have to agree to their plans; it just means that you're willing to hold a space for their perspective. And that you're willing to see the potentially good intent behind a plan or idea you may not like.

> **Discernment truly is the challenge of the twenty-first century.**

Discernment truly is the challenge of the twenty-first century. There are millions of ideas, and everyone is screaming that theirs is the best. If we can discipline our minds to seek out the core truths behind the surface shouting, we can rise above the either/or thinking that has so limited us in the past.

It's not about compromising our ideals, and you don't need to try to partner with someone who doesn't truly want to make things better. But just because their version of better looks different than ours, we needn't judge their intentions as less than honorable.

It's much easier to give people the thumbs-up or thumbs-down than it is to discern the truth behind their imperfect thoughts. But how much have we cost ourselves on both an individual and a global level because we mistook ill-conceived or incomplete agendas for true malevolence?

When we express moral indignation over the imperfect solutions being presented by others, we aren't solving problems; we're contributing to them. When we begin assuming ill intent, all open-minded discussion stops. Yet if we can pause and try to discern the true intent behind someone's thinking we will likely find a truth we can support.

Discernment takes longer than judging because it requires us to give people the benefit of the doubt and to consider the full context of situations, and also to hold multiple perspectives in our minds at the same time.

Choosing discernment over judgment isn't easy because it often means putting your own emotions, prejudice, and ideas aside and directing your efforts toward uncovering the truths on the other side—truths we may not want to hear from people we may not like.

But do you want to be the person who is good at telling other people why they're wrong? Or do you want to be the person who is able to discern the truths of others and invite them to bring their perspective to the party?

Judgment is easy; discernment is much more challenging. But if we can learn to discern and honor each other's truths, there is no limit to what we can accomplish.

Elevate Others

*How to Change the Way Other People Think and
Why You Should Even Bother to Try*

It's easier for a leader to blame the problem on
someone else than it is for them to solve it.
—ALEX MCLEOD, AGE ELEVEN

We often believe that the best leaders are the people who can come up with the best solutions, or who can articulate the most compelling thoughts. In reality, the best leaders are usually the people who ask the best questions.

The above quote is from my daughter. It was in response to a question her fifth-grade teacher asked the class about Adolph Hitler. The teacher had assigned the kids a project to answer the question, "Why did the Germans follow Adolph Hitler?" In groups of four or five, they researched the economic, social, and religious issues of the time, and the conclusion that my daughter's team reached was that the Germans were cold, hungry, and poor, and because of that they were susceptible to a leader who preyed on their fears, and pointed to a scapegoat. Creating a plan for the county to solve its own problems would have been difficult and challenging. In an environment of fear and suffering, it was easier for a hate-based leader to blame their problems on a small subgroup within and get the nation fired up against a common enemy. Or at least that's the way the kids described it to me.

Keep in mind these are a bunch of fifth graders.

When I saw the finished project, it was a large three-fold science-project-style cardboard presentation poster, with their simple conclusion, "It is easier for a leader to blame the problems on someone else than it is to ask society to solve them" written on a notecard taped to the center of the poster board. Surrounding it were all the facts documenting the horrific state of the Germany people prior to the start of World War II. The miserable job market, the falling value of their currency, the shortage of food, all neatly summarized in gold pen on little blue note cards pasted on either side of their big answer.

I was amazed. With less than three hours to research it, a bunch of ten- and eleven-year-olds were able to discern the reason behind much of the war, terror, and killing on this planet. One of the world's greatest truths has now been posted on a piece of cardboard in the back of an elementary school classroom.

So why do a group of fifth graders seem to have more insight into human affairs than many adults?

Their leader asked the right question.

I might like to believe that my own child is brilliant, and trust me, she is. But the five other project teams came up with pretty much the same answer that hers did. I think the one who is really demonstrating the big brains here is the teacher.

With one simple question, she recast the entire dialogue, and prompted a group of fifth graders to think more deeply than half the adults I know. She got them to see both the forest and the trees, and she elevated their thinking in a way that will stick with them for the rest of their lives.

This is what it means to be a real leader. It's someone who goes beyond telling people what to think, but who instead teaches them *how to think*. And this is what every single one of us has the capacity to do in our own lives, no matter what our circumstances or role.

Elevating the Conversation

It doesn't matter whether we want to create world peace, a successful business, a happy family, or all three, we cannot do it alone. If we want to create different paradigms, in our relationships or on a bigger scale, we must find a way to get our fellow humans involved in the process.

Just as our best teachers have had the patience to meet us where we are, so too must we have the patience to meet others where they are. If we're frustrated by the way they think, we need to honor their good intentions and help them illuminate a new path. If we believe that they're limiting themselves and others with their narrow-mindedness, we need to love them enough to show them a way out of it.

But you can't just tell people to become more intelligent and less judgmental; if that worked we would have all gotten smarter a long time ago. If we truly want to help others elevate their thinking, we are going to have work through the process alongside them.

And when it comes to elevating other people's thinking, there's no one who provides a better lesson than the fifth-grade teacher.

Despite working in an environment where an ability to regurgitate information is what her students will be tested on, and what her performance will be graded on, and what will determine her future pay, this teacher decided that she was going to elevate the dialogue and teach conceptual thinking, whether it was on the county-mandated syllabus or not.

If she can do it with twenty-five fifth graders, you can do it with your spouse, your coworker, and even your narrow-minded neighbor.

This particular teacher (Ginny Arndt, a Georgia educator who proves that public schools in the South do more than just teach kids how to conjugate the word *ain't*) achieved what so many other leaders struggle with.

She ignited a level of critical thinking that enabled her kids to see both the forest and the trees, and she delivered short-term results, while at the same time setting her team up for even better performance over the long haul.

Her students will remember the facts about WWII. In all likelihood, they will probably remember them even better than the kids whose teachers spent long hours trying to cram information into their students' heads. Because she asked the kids a big picture question, they now have a context for the facts, and the information is more likely to be retained because it has more meaning.

Big Questions, Little Stories

If you want someone—be it your spouse, employees, constituents, or friends—to break out of an either/or mind-set and to see a bigger picture than the one they are currently holding, there are two incredibly effective techniques that you can use to unlock their mind: big questions and little stories.

Big questions expand our intellect, and little stories expand our emotions. One is about the head, the other is about the heart, and if you want to change the way people think, you need to incorporate both.

The kids in my daughter's class were asked a big question. But they discovered the answer through little stories about how a chocolate bar cost four thousand marks and how German kids played with big blocks of useless money.

The teacher's big question prompted the research, and the little stories provided a meaningful anchor for the facts.

Asking questions helps people self-discover larger truths, but it's the little stories that make the information stick. This is another duality we must master if we want to elevate others.

The Doorbell Dynamic

It's always a challenge to keep ourselves and others grounded in the big picture. Our lives can get so frantic with so many tasks to do and so much information coming in, that we often fail to see our day-to-day actions in their full context.

How many times have you found yourself frustrated because

your spouse, coworkers, boss, employees, or kids could only see one little piece of something and didn't understand how their behavior and actions were affecting everything and everyone else?

In our family we call it the doorbell dynamic, and there's a little story that explains it.

My parents remodeled a house a few years back. It was an old boxy 1960s split-level home on a lake. They bought it because the lake was beautiful, it was near the grandkids, and the price was right. It needed a lot of work. They pretty much gutted the entire interior. They had an architect do a plan, and a decorator helped pick out the colors and accoutrements. After months of work, the result was an open, relaxed space, with windows on almost every wall showcasing the lake and nature.

The house was almost finished when the guy came to put the new doorbell in. My stepmother wasn't there when he installed it, but she arrived home to discover that the ringer part of the bell had been hung directly in the center of the only decent-size wall on the entire first floor.

The only wall where you could put a mirror or art or piece of furniture now had a little five by five white plastic box right slap in the middle of it.

Apparently, when standing in the middle of all that glass and openness, the doorbell man was drawn to the largest vacant canvas available, and because doorbells were clearly important to him, he centered his handiwork in the most prominent spot in the room for all the world to see. So upon entering the beautiful architect-created, decorator-designed home, the first thing you saw was the large white plastic doorbell device hanging smack in the middle of the sage green wall adjacent to the forest green front door with side transoms.

After calling the doorbell man back to her home to reposition the bell in a more discreet location, my stepmother discovered how much care and thought had gone into his plan. "I could see that this was a nice place and that you were obviously real particular," he said, "so I made double sure that I had it exactly centered. It's not just centered side to side, ma'am, it's centered floor to ceiling, too."

Alas, yet another well-intentioned person trying to do their best work yet completely oblivious to the fact that their job is part of a larger project.

How many of us have done the same thing, or at least observed it in others? The specialist doctor treats the one component of the illness, but neglects to address the myriad of other connected problems that are making the patient miserable. The politician pursues an agenda that is important to one vocal subset of his constituents but fails to consider the impact it might have on others. The accounts receivable person collects the money on time, yet so angers the customer that they refuse to do business with us again. The volunteer recruiter finds enough warm bodies to man all the booths for Family Fun Day, but her strong-arm recruiting tactics are so off-putting that people feel like virtual prisoners behind the snow cone machine. I take my family to France and get angry because my kids won't "get out of bed, so we can beat the crowd and look at the damn Monet before everybody else shows up," and I forget that the whole purpose of the trip was family togetherness.

Most of us don't set out intending to create problems for others, but our inability to see beyond on our own nose, and a tendency to hold a myopic view of everything that pertains to us, frequently causes our best intentions to fall short of the mark. An inability to see the big picture, or even just momentarily losing sight of it, is what prompts people to defend narrow agendas.

However, if we want to elevate the dialogue about a family issue, business problem, or political argument, we have to be able to get people to lift their minds and consider additional information that is not currently in their line of sight.

The secret is to enlighten people about the big picture without criticizing where they are today. Said another way, you want to show the doorbell guy how much you appreciate his good intentions while at the same time graciously help him self-discover that hanging a piece of white plastic in the middle of your foyer might not be the best approach.

It would be nice if we could simply tell the myopic doorbell hangers what the big picture looks like, and they would immediately understand, and retain that information until the end of time. I'm frequently guilty of assuming that whenever I encounter someone who disagrees with me, all I need to do is enlighten them with a larger vision and they will easily be able to discern how our two perspectives can be assimilated. At times that may work.

More often than not, we're going to have to do a little strategic thinking if we want to be the catalyst who creates the "aha" moment for others.

Ask *And* Tell

It is not without coincidence that religions teach lessons through stories. Or that good speakers tell stories to illustrate their points, or that business and self-help books include case studies that we can all relate to. Facts are forgettable, but stories are not.

Here's how the combination of big questions and little stories can help you elevate someone's thinking.

Let's say I'm complaining about my crazy narrow-minded neighbor, and I'm going on and on about how awful she is, and you're tired of listening to me whine (who wouldn't be?). You can remind me that we're all flawed and fabulous, or you can go deeper, and redirect the conversation in a way that prompts me to think rather than just respond. You needn't agree or disagree with my assessment of the problem. But if you ask a simple question like "Why do you think she behaves that way?" or "How do you think she came to this place in her life?" it may prompt me to consider the full context of the situation. And there's a chance I may be willing to look beyond the flawed label that my either/or brain has slapped on her file folder. I may even pause to consider the roots of our disagreements from her perspective. Of course, I may also tell you that she acts like that because she's an evil witch and that the planet would be better off without her.

But, heavy sigh, nobody said changing the world was going to be easy.

If you want to encourage someone to hold a more compassionate, open view, questions can prompt them to reflect, and stories can provide them with a new context for considering the information. Telling me a story about the time my narrow-minded neighbor gave food to the poor, or even better, asking me if I can think of any situations where she did something nice will cause me to make a small mental shift. I might not change my opinion of her overnight, but if you can plant a seed that causes me to think about her just a little bit differently, you will be helping me create more peace in my life. Who knows what impact that may have on the people around me.

I call them big questions because you ask them with the intent of prompting people to step back and look at a bigger picture. The stories need to be little in that they are small, personal, and easy to understand.

Going back to our well-intended doorbell hanger. How might things have gone differently if his boss, the general contractor, had ever asked him, "What impact do you think we have on people's lives?" What if one day when they were on their lunch break, the contractor had said, "You know we work on about twenty houses a year, and I often wonder how all the people live in them after we're gone."

Or what if the first time he had sent the doorbell man out for a job, the contractor had gone with him and said, "Whenever I install something, one of the questions I always like to ask myself is, 'How do I think this room will be used?' and then I try to figure out where's the least obtrusive place I can put the hardware so it won't get in the way." Or if he had told him a funny story about someone trying to arrange all their family photos around the white doorbell chimer.

The doorbell man might respond with, "Buddy, are you nuts? I just install doorbells, now leave me alone and let me do my job in peace." Or he might find himself thinking back on the conversation the next time he goes into someone's house.

There's no magic order, but people usually need both the questions and the stories to lift their thinking.

Criticizing Versus Inviting

People want to be part of something bigger than themselves; in fact, they yearn for it. Much of human angst is simply due to lack of purpose. People who can master the art of asking big questions and telling little stories help people see that they are part of something special, and how their efforts combine to make a greater whole.

For example, you can beat your uber-consuming, SUV-driving, non-recycling in-laws about the head with all the facts about global warming. Or you can ask them, "What do you think happens to all the trash?" "Where do you think we should put it?" Or "Why do you think so many people care so much about the environment?" It's probably going to prompt them to think a little bit, rather than just reacting to your criticism of their gas hog. If you get one of their precious grandkids to tell them a little story about how excited they are that their school is now recycling, so they will still have a planet to live on, all the better.

You have to elevate someone's perspective before you can expect them to change their actions. Once they acknowledge that there's a larger issue (planet in peril) then you can ask (nicely), "Would you be interested in a list of small things that you can do this afternoon?" Who knows, you might even be able to get them to change out their lightbulbs, and Al Gore will send them a thank-you.

People would rather be invited to part of the solution than be criticized for being part of the problem. Asking big questions prompts them to think rather than react.

However, like all other techniques I've suggested, asking the big questions works best if you can hold a good intention in your heart, and if you ask from the perspective of actually wanting to know their answer.

Locked and Loaded Questions

Big questions are meant to be thought provoking, not accusatory or manipulative.

If you ask questions with an unspoken "Duh, why don't you already know this?" at the end, people will probably respond negatively because they'll be responding to your unspoken message.

When you're trying to ignite more enlightened thinking, the way you phrase things is pretty important. Sales and leadership classes teach questioning skills; in most cases it's done with an honest intent to help people better connect. But there's one style of questions that, although frequently suggested by experts, almost never works. It's the locked and loaded questions like, "Wouldn't you look great driving this car up to your class reunion?" Or the ever popular, "If I could find a way to solve all your problems you sure would want to sign on the dotted line, wouldn't you now?" Not that I haven't attempted such obviously manipulative behavior myself, as I so often demonstrate with my favorite parenting question, "What can you do to prevent this from happening again?" asked with a sarcastic smile and a big dose of I-told-you so attitude thrown in.

These types of comments may have a question mark on the end, but the real intent is to get the other person to do what we want as quickly as possible. My husband refers to it as the how-can-I-criticize-you-in-the-form-of-a-question game. It's kind of like the *Jeopardy!* home game.

Alex, I'll take improving your husband's eating habits for $500, please. And the question is, "Bob, how do you think eating three chili cheese dogs for lunch is going to help you lose weight?"

Locked and loaded questions don't work because they are nothing more than "When are you going to see the wisdom of my solution" commentary. However, mind-opening questions tend to be more along the lines of "Why do you think we are having this problem?" or "How might we approach this differently?" They're the most effective when you can set aside any attachment you may have to the person reaching a particular conclusion.

One style of questions is trying to validate your own conclusions, while the other style is prompting the other person to discern some core truths about the entire situation.

Once Upon a Triangle

Let's say you're in the middle of a no-holds-barred war of a budget meeting, or you're trying to mediate a fight between your kids. How do you put things on pause and get both sides to consider the big picture and find some truths in what their nemesis is saying?

Simple, you use the triangle. You can do it subtly, validating the information on both sides, using skillful questions to try to steer them toward their higher truth.

Or you can do what I do. If the situation is more urgent, say for example the IT guy is threatening to strangle the operations manager, whistle loudly to get everyone's attention, get out a piece of paper or a flip chart, draw a triangle on it, stand up, and say, "This department has one truth, this department has another, but as a company we need to be at the top of triangle. I don't want you to water down your perspective, nor do I expect you to compromise. I want us to get to the place where we can get the full value of what both of you are offering.

"We're going to solve this problem, and we're going to solve it together. So let's see if we can discern the most important truth on either side before the end of the day, because I don't think the CEO is going to be very happy if he has to foot the bill for us to battle this out for another twenty-four hours."

Sometimes life is too short for subtlety.

However, even if you're blunt, impatient, and time clock–driven you can still take the time to craft good questions. In the long run, it makes the process of assimilating agendas and truths go much faster.

Instead of using narrow *what* and *when* questions, try opening the dialogue with more expansive *how* or *why* questions. This will help you uncover the core truths behind the proposed solutions with less drama. For example, instead of asking the IT people what they think the problem is, try asking them how it is affecting them and why the company needs to solve it. *What* and *when* questions tend to keep them stuck in regurgitating their solutions, whereas *how* and *why* questions often prompt them to pause and think more deeply. (You can download the Triangle of Truth Meeting Prep Sheet off our site.)

This method also works with quarreling children. If you ask them what they want, they'll tell you that they want their sister to move to Mars so they can have all the ice cream and TV time for themselves. If you draw the Triangle and ask them how it feels to be on their side on the line, you will inevitably discover some emotions that you can validate, emotions that in no way conflict with the feelings on the other side.

If you're surprised by me comparing bickering department heads to sparring siblings arguing over something as trivial as who let their foot drift across the invisible line down the middle of the backseat, all I can say is, you've obviously never had to manage a budget meeting. The truth is, whether we're five or we're fifty, we're all human and we often fall into the same behavior patterns. We just gussy it up a little bit as we get older.

An important thing to note here: You don't have to have a clear idea about what the top of the Triangle might look like in order to start using the process. In fact, sometimes it's better if you don't. Stepping up to lead the process doesn't mean that you have to know the answers; it just means that you're willing to help people discern the truth on both sides. This is in and of itself challenging, because people will cling to their solutions. Asking people to step back and look at the larger picture is hard when they're knee-deep in their own perspectives. But if you can ask big picture questions, you'll get some big picture truths on the table, and you'll have a better chance of co-creating a solution that has buy in from both sides.

It's also important to note that you don't have to be the official leader to be the one who initiates the process. Even if you're one of the people who is arguing, you can take a breath, and have the wherewithal to step back, and say, "Hey, let's take a pause here, we all want to be successful, instead of arguing over whose solution is best, perhaps there is a way we can integrate them. How might we do that?" (Said with an open face and a nonjudgmental smile.)

They might not come up with the answers right away, or even that day. But it will cause them to pause and think.

Why Some Stories Work Better Than Others

Did you ever notice how in those Save the Children ads they almost never show you a big field of starving children—instead, they just show you one? You rarely see masses of children; it's usually just one little doe-eyed, sweet child. That's because one little hungry child touches our heartstrings and sticks in our memory more than a million would.

This is one of the secrets to making a connection with people, and influencing their thinking. If you tell someone there are millions of starving kids, we need to solve this problem, it feels impersonal, and also insurmountable. But if you show them a photo of sweet little Rosa, with her beseeching brown eyes, and tell them her personal story, describing what it feels like to live each day in hunger, so hungry that you can't even walk to school, and then ask, How can we get Rosa a better dinner tomorrow night? they're much more likely to take it as a call to action.

Personal stories help people get out of their own head, and see a perspective different than their own, which is why they're a great technique for helping people rise above an either/or mind-set.

One of the frustrations that many of us face when we're try- ing to solve a business battle or a family squabble or some other conflict is that people get so stuck on their view, they can't see anything else. Which is why we have turf wars, and families argue over who is supposed to do what. Everyone is focused on their own part, but because they don't put their actions in the context of the larger organization, they miss opportunities. They don't interact as well with the other groups as they could, and they don't fully understand how their work impacts others.

This is where stories can help. I often use stories in my consulting work, and we build them into our Triangle of Truth workshops because it's an incredibly effective and easy technique for elevating people's thinking. For example, if a company makes widgets and the people who make part A of the widget don't understand how their work affects the people who make part B of the widget or how the customers ultimately use the widgets, they're not going to be very motivated to do much more than slap their parts on and send it down the line. And if problems arise, or questions come up, they're not going to be able to make good decisions, because they don't give much thought to how their part affects the greater whole.

If you can, tell them a story about what happens when part A of the widget winds up in front of Joe, who assembles part B. Tell them how when part A shows up perfectly formed and on time, Joe gets to make it home in time for dinner with his family, but when it shows up late and incomplete, poor Joe has to work all night, and might wind up getting divorced as a result, they're probably going to pay more attention to how they put together part A. And if you tell them a story about the widget going home with a particular customer, and how they used it, and how it impacted their lives, they're going to be more inclined to work with Joe and the rest of the team in department B, to create a better end result. Suddenly their work becomes meaningful. You've put their tasks into the context of a larger story. And that's one of the secrets of getting people to see both sides of the Triangle. Stories help them see the bigger picture *And* the other side of the Triangle at the same time.

Telling stories keeps people grounded in a vision larger than themselves, making them much more willing to assimilate their agenda with others' instead of defending why their goals alone should rule.

Remember the pharmaceutical sales rep from the earlier chapter who every day held a vision in her heart of the now symptom-free grandmother? If you want people to see the larger picture, sometimes you have to be the one who provides them with the stories. You can eliminate a lot of single-agenda back and forth bickering if you continually use stories to remind people of the larger goals.

Stories help people see another person's perspective, and it's a technique you can use in a multitude of situations. Let's say you're at an impasse over household chores with your child or spouse and screaming at them about how they should do their part isn't getting much buy in.

Tell a story about how you came home from a business trip and saw the filthy kitchen and the mountain of laundry piled in the foyer, and sat down on the sofa and cried your eyes out because your life felt like one big, long to-do list and everywhere you turned was another task. Your feelings are probably going to garner more empathy than a rant about their failings.

But be careful with "woe is me" stories. Yes, you do want people to see your side of things, but if you're really trying to elevate a conversation and move beyond either/or, you need to make sure you understand their side of the Triangle before you tell the tearjerker story about yours.

Stories aren't meant to be manipulative; they're meant to help break people out of the brain-lock that keeps them stuck on their perspective.

How Sharing Perspectives Unlocks Creativity

One of the problems with either/or thinking is that it stifles creative thought. Business consultant Joe Calloway says that he sees the problem all the time when he works with people on innovation. One of the techniques that he uses to help people get unstuck is to get one group to solve another group's problem.

He describes a recent scenario with a client in which he took their twenty-two VPs, put them into groups of four, and assigned each team one of the other teams' priorities, so they were charged with brainstorming and problem-solving for a group outside their normal job function. We use a similar technique in our programs and it accomplishes two things. First, you get new ideas on the table, because as nonexperts who aren't stakeholders in the priority, the groups don't limit their thinking as much as they would had they been dealing with the issue for years.

There's another more subtle shift. Asking someone to step into the role of another person gets them into the habit of looking at things from multiple angles. By working on another person's problem or challenge, people are

> It's amazing how much less bickering you get when people have to live in another person's shoes for a while.

required to really think about what it might be like to work in that environment, or meet those requirements or live that life. It's amazing how much less bickering you get when people have to live in another person's shoes for a while.

But the swap technique isn't just for businesses. You can use the same process with your kids or family members. If two people are arguing over something, ask them to take a break and then come back and explain the problem from the other person's perspective. You might not create peace all at once, but at least you will have elevated the dialogue.

Elevating other people is about creating an environment that prompts them to seek deeper truths so that they can reach more enlightened conclusions, and get a little closer to the top of the Triangle.

Beyond Balance

Balance is a popular buzzword. People want a balanced life, organizations are expected to balance their budgets, and our country was created with a system of checks and balances. There's nothing wrong with balance per se. But we need to be careful that in our attempts to balance things, we don't water down the best of what we've got, and that we don't allow the goal of balance to keep us stuck in continual conflict.

I bring up the subject of balance in the context of helping others elevate their thinking, because if you've ever been in charge of something, be it a family, department, or huge organization, you've no doubt found yourself having to balance multiple needs, goals, and agendas.

One department head wants to do one thing, the other wants to go in a different direction; one kid wants to go to the pool, the other prefers the movie; one committee thinks the group should focus on their project, the other committee believes theirs in the most important.

It can make you feel like you've got your head in a vise as you try to mediate between the warring factions. You find yourself keeping score, and trying to remember who you sided with last time, just so that you don't get accused of playing favorites. (And we wonder why some people don't like to be in charge.)

When conflicting priorities clash against each other, you'll often hear well-intended, thoughtful people say, "What we really need here is balance." That's certainly a kinder, more gracious attitude than those who would say, "Just shut up and do what I say." What frequently happens is that when a manager, leader, parent, or committee chair tries to balance the needs of different people or groups, their well-intended efforts actually keep people stuck inside the conflict.

When you assume that it's your job to balance all the agendas against each another, you're assuming sole responsibility for the big picture. You are in effect saying, "It's OK for you all to only see one part of things because I'm going to be the one who assimilates all the goals." This sets up a situation where people often remain in continual disagreement, because they've never been required to fully consider any perspective beyond their own.

Here's how it often plays out. Person A has one agenda, person B has another, they can't get along, and either because you're their boss, or parent, or peacemaking friend, they bring the problem to you. You then try to help them work out some sort of compromise, balancing the needs and goals of person A against the needs and goals of person B. You try to show person A how person B feels, and you try to get person B to see where person A is coming from, they both soften a little, they give on a few issues, agree to meet in the middle, and you think the problem is solved. Until they're back in your office the next week bickering over a similar problem.

How do I know? Because it's happened to me about a million times.

The reason they're staying stuck in conflict is that while you may have helped them see the other side's perspective for a moment, they haven't yet taken full responsibility for lifting their own thinking. They don't have to think outside their perspective because every time a conflict arises, they take the problem to you.

But we do ourselves, and our organizations, and our families a grave disservice when we try to short-circuit the process for others. If you really want people to be able to move beyond either/or thinking, modeling the process is the best first step. But at a certain point, you want them to be able to do it on their own.

If you find yourself playing mediator a bit more often than you'd like, it's probably time to take the big questions, little stories technique to the next level. Instead of just using the techniques to help them see the other side of the Triangle or to help them hold a vision of the something bigger than themselves, ask them how they might do that for someone else.

If they're complaining to you about a conflict, try asking how they might help the other person see the big picture. What stories could *you* tell that would help them (the person you're complaining about) understand the other side of the Triangle? What questions can *you* ask that might prompt them to think bigger than just either/or?

Trying to balance the needs of many, or even just a few, may keep the peace for a while, but until you teach people to initiate the process on their own, they will continue to stay stuck.

A Special Note for Leaders

Each and every one of us has the capacity to influence the thinking of the people around us, so in that sense, we're all leaders. We owe it to ourselves and our organizations and families to show up as our best selves and try to elevate others whenever we can. But I'd like to provide a few specific thoughts for those who are in an official leadership capacity, be it as a parent, project manager, or CEO, or those who want to be in a leadership capacity at some point in the future.

One of the biggest challenges of being a leader is overcoming your own prejudices and biases. The world is filled with companies that went south because the fiscally prudent CEO didn't pay enough attention to sales and marketing, or ad agencies that went belly-up because the creative genius founder didn't put systems in place to make sure the other creatives got their work in on time, or families that flounder in chaos or are stifled under militaristic rule because mom or dad had a predisposition for one style of leading.

There's a Chinese proverb that says, "Any virtue taken to an extreme is a vice."

If you're predisposed toward a particular style, or set of ideas, or a certain job function or discipline, that predisposition has the potential to blind you to the other side of the Triangle. Which might be OK, if there's always someone around who is willing to challenge you. But in many instances, we find ourselves in situations where people are not inclined to go against our wishes, or we've filled our team with people just like ourselves, so we're all blind to the other side.

For example, imagine you're on a team in which nine of the ten people are sunny-side up optimists. In walks Eeyore, who fills in all the facts about why your plan might go wrong. You might be inclined to roll your eyes and get annoyed at Mr. Wet Blanket for raining on your parade. But just because you don't like his approach doesn't mean he's wrong.

You can't allow a negative person to derail everyone else, but sometimes you need to let Mr. Wet Blanket share his story. Because if you don't, he's going to give up and go away, and you'll wind up missing what may have been a very valuable perspective.

Sometimes people really are just bellyachers; but if you're the leader, it's your job to get the real truths out on the table, so that you and your team have the best information to work from. Even if they happen to be truths that you might be inclined to steer away from yourself.

Good leaders do a double check on the people who agree with them to make sure they're not just sucking up. They do a triple check on the people whose opinions are different, because in all likelihood that's the perspective they need to hear the most.

It's challenging as a leader to know when to step in and when to back off. It's not the leader's job to solve all the problems. It's the leader's job to set other people up for success.

But you can't expect people to be motivated to solve problems they don't believe exist.

I can certainly browbeat my family into cleaning up the house before company comes, but if they don't see any inherent value in it, the pizza boxes are going to be all over the floor again two days after Grandma leaves.

If you want the people around you to do more than just follow orders, you need to help them see not only the consequences of a problem, but also prompt them to look at the roots of them.

The problems of either/or thinking are many, but they're rooted in an inability see the big picture.

However, what would happen if every parent taught their child, when faced with a problem or crisis, to pause and consider the root issues? Ask yourself, what kind of thinking and systems contributed to this problem and how might I look at this from a different perspective so that I can get a different result in the future?

What if corporations were filled with people who could not only accomplish their assigned tasks today, but who could also see them in the context of the larger mission? People who in meetings and in their day-to-day actions were constantly look-ing beyond the either/ors of the presenting problems, and who were committed to co-creating success with their colleagues.

Where might our planet be, if all our policy makers and politicos challenged the public to look at the root causes of our problems, and not succumb to the ideologically based reactive solutions that have hindered us in the past?

People are yearning for leadership that calls us into being our better selves. If you ask people the right questions, and share your stories, sometimes their responses will amaze you.

Good leadership is a lesson in assimilating dualities, and helping others assimilate dualities as well. You have to get infor-mation flowing from the top down, and also from the bottom up. You need to create an environment of rigorous discipline as well as creative thought. You must be firm in your convictions, yet compassionate in your approach. You need to speak with authority, and listen with humility. You must help people hold a clear vision of where they're going, and also encourage them to be open to what the world serves up.

The Triangle model can help you master the dualities of leadership, and it can help you elevate the thoughts and minds of the people around you. While the challenges of leadership are many, for those willing to serve, the rewards are infinite. To serve as a leader is to be granted the opportunity to influence the way other people think and live. Whether you do it in the privacy of your own home or on an international stage, when you influence others, you're changing the world, even if it's just a little bit at a time. It might not feel significant while you're doing it, but every time you elevate the thoughts of another person, you make a difference to us all.

Why We're All Called to Lead

The Triangle of Truth is a tool that can be used by anyone. It can be utilized by leaders, both official and unofficial, to elevate the thinking of the people around them and their organizations. It can be used in a creative capacity, as a tool for assimilating multiple thoughts and ideas. And it can be used to solve conflicts big and small.

I use the Triangle model almost every single day, with clients, with my family, and when I'm working on projects. Seeing both sides of things and figuring out how to integrate multiple perspectives has become part of who I am.

But the most meaningful experience for me is when other people use the model themselves. When they're not dependent on me to facilitate the process, but when they can start asking the questions, connecting with stories, and making a proactive effort to seek out and hold a space for perspectives other than their own. That's why we offer so many free tools on our website, because we want to make it accessible and easy. When people teach others how to use the Triangle model, I, too, feel as though I've helped make the world a little bit better place.

> If you want the people around you to rise above either/or thinking and be able to assimilate multiple thoughts and ideas, you have the power to start the process.

If you want the people around you to rise above either/or thinking and be able to assimilate multiple thoughts and ideas, you have the power to start the process.

Whenever someone asks thought-provoking questions, or connects with a story, or even announces to their team or spouse that they're going to put their own perspective aside so that they can focus on the other person, everything starts to change.

When we make the decision to elevate our own thinking it has a ripple effect on everyone around us. When we decide to step into leadership and apply our best intentions toward helping someone else rise above an either/or paradigm, we not only do them a favor, we help ourselves as well.

Because like it or not, we're all connected, and the mind-set of each individual person contributes to the greater whole. It's challenging to rise above our either/or instincts, but when one person makes the effort to think in terms of *And*, others often naturally follow.

The lesson of the Triangle is simple: We're better together than we are apart.

When you move out of the realm of either/or and open your mind to the possibility of *And*, you change the way you approach the world. You open the door to new ways of solving problems, and you create a space that enables others to think more creatively as well.

The top of the Triangle isn't perfection. It's peace, peace within ourselves, peace in our families, peace in our organizations, and, dare I say it, perhaps even peace in the world.

We've spent a lot of time on this planet fighting and trying to get our way. Either/or thinking has caused us to turn against each other time and time again.

But perhaps we're finally ready to embrace a new model.

Be the Peace

How to Solve the Conflict in Our Head by
Changing the Spirit in Our Heart

All truths are easy to understand once they are
discovered: The point is to discover them.
—GALILEO GALILEI

Galileo Galilei was jailed as a heretic for having the audacity to suggest that the earth moved around the sun. The man whose groundbreaking work marked the dawn of modern astronomy was convicted of heresy in 1663 because he had the gall to tell the people of Rome that the sun did not actually rise and set upon them.

He's hardly the first person, nor will he be that last, to get into trouble for telling people that they are not the center of the Universe.

Galileo's theory, known as heliocentrism, was denounced by the Church and during his trial he was instructed "to abandon this doctrine, not to teach it to others, and not to defend it."

He was convicted and sentenced to life imprisonment, a sentence later commuted to house arrest for the rest of his life.

Which just goes to show you how far some people will go to prove themselves right.

When the controversy around him was heating up, Galileo wrote a letter to Johannes Kepler, a German mathematician, in which he expressed his frustration that the people who opposed his discoveries refused to even look through his telescope.

The truth was right there in front of them, yet they couldn't bear to see it. Galileo's new truth conflicted with their long-held beliefs, so they not only ignored it, they publicly denounced it.

I started off this book by telling you that I wanted to answer two simple questions: Why do we drive each other crazy, and how can we create peace?

The answer is shockingly simple: We drive each other nuts because we believe that we're the only one who's right.

The belief that one person's truth is the only truth is what causes couples to split up, businesses to flounder, countries to divide, and religions to make war on one another, killing people in the name of the divine.

But the real truth is, we don't know everything. We don't know the whole truth about science, we don't know the whole truth about religion, we don't know the whole truth about government, we don't know the whole truth about business, we don't know the whole truth about families, we don't know the whole truth about each other, and we don't even know the whole truth about ourselves.

It's not our truths that cause the problems, it's our belief in their exclusivity.

It's not our truths that cause the problems, it's our belief in their exclusivity.

Until we admit that we are not the sole purveyors of the truth, we will forever be stuck in one-dimensional thinking. Either/or, I'm right so you must be wrong, thinking causes us problems everywhere from the bedroom to the boardroom and beyond. It's a paradigm that has been in existence since the dawn of time and it plays out on a global level as well as a personal one. But it's a paradigm we can change.

Because it's not our differences that divide us, it's our inability to manage them.

Conflict itself isn't a bad thing. Some of our greatest breakthroughs and advances have occurred when two seemingly conflicting perspectives rubbed up against each other. Conflict is merely different ideas and perspectives coming to the surface. It's the insistence that other people's ideas are wrong that keeps us trapped in endless go-nowhere debates.

Conflict can actually be a catalyst for creativity. Yet if we believe that our only options are to squelch it or win it we will continue to argue and fight, stuck in the belief that my truth is more accurate than yours, and that if I'm right, you must be wrong.

Either/or thinking stifles our compassion. And when we lose our compassion, we lose our ability to love and create, which is our true purpose on this planet.

It not without coincidence that all the great religions of this world speak of love and unity. It is a sacred truth that binds us together. It is only narrow, literal interpretations of these truths that cause us to bicker and fight.

The Triangle of Truth is an intellectual model, but it has spiritual implications. The problem has never really been in our heads; it's in our hearts. And the only way we can solve problems of the heart is with a healing of the spirit.

I once read a parenting book that suggested that in an ideal circumstance, a child is raised to believe that they are incredibly special, but no more special than anyone else. This is our real problem; we cannot imagine a world where one person's specialness does not come at the expense of another. We've been told that we are marvelous, and we've also been told that we're no better than anyone else. Our inability to assimilate these two truths causes a sadness of spirit that plays out on every level.

We're reluctant to believe that we are amazing and that we have a higher purpose. Or if we do believe that we've been chosen, it is unfathomable to us that everyone else has been chosen as well.

Until we embrace the idea that we are all the chosen ones, that every person with whom we share this planet has just as much right to be here as we do, and that their thoughts, needs, goals, and desires are no less important than ours, we will always be stuck. Stuck in the belief that your specialness comes at the expense of mine.

How many more souls must we sacrifice on the altar of limited thinking before we finally realize, we're all in this together? Haven't we wallowed in fear and narrow-mindedness for long enough?

We can continue to live in fear, and divide the world up into either/ors. Or we can step into the light of love and see the truth about who we are—people who were meant to love and be loved. And who know that your truth never diminishes mine.

It is no longer enough for us to be peacekeepers; it is time for us to be peacemakers. Peacekeepers keep conflict under wraps. Peacemakers know how to assimilate our conflicting perspectives into something amazing. Your truth plus my truth equals a new reality for us all.

You've probably figured it out by now. This was more than just a book about how you manage conflict, or innovate at work, or get along with your crazy neighbor. It's a lesson in how we can better learn to love.

It is time for us to love and be loved, with all of our heart and soul. Because when we learn to love ourselves and to love each other, that is when we will finally create peace.

You really are the one we've been waiting for. We all are. You are the shining light of truth, and your words have power beyond belief. On the day that you were born the world rejoiced, because we knew that you were sent here to do something very special.

You are the one. You are a peacemaker, and for that, we are truly grateful.

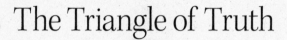

The Triangle of Truth

Seven Principles

1. **Embrace *And*.** Lift your mind above either/or instincts to embrace the full flawed and fabulous duality of the human condition.

2. **Make peace with ambiguity.** Choose love over fear to face the facts with faith, even in the face of uncertain outcomes.

3. **Hold space for their perspective.** Put your own agenda on pause to eliminate the false barrier between you and others.

4. **Seek higher ground.** Break past the comfort and convenience of false choices by thinking beyond holding your ground or compromising in the middle.

5. **Discern intent.** Withhold judgments about imperfect solutions in order to discern the inherent truths behind them.

6. **Elevate others.** Ask big questions and share little stories to elevate intellect and touch emotions.

7. **Be the peace.** Embrace differences with your head and your heart to become a peacemaker in work, love, and life.

The Triangle of Truth

- Be the peace
- Elevate others
- Discern intent
- Seek higher ground
- Hold space for their perspective
- Make peace with ambiguity
- Embrace *And*

The Triangle of Truth

Results

Since the first printing of *The Triangle of Truth*, I've done keynotes and workshops around the world, and our company, McLeod & More Inc., has run programs for sales organizations, leadership teams, franchise groups, and educators.

We've taught the Triangle of Truth concepts and skills to everyone from salespeople to CEOs to volunteers and teachers. And the number one question we get is, "I'm willing to use the model, but what if they won't budge?"

The simple answer is: It still works.

After working with hundreds of organizations and individuals, we can definitively say beyond a shadow of a doubt that when one person changes their approach, the entire dynamic of a situation changes, and you get a completely different outcome. It's not just about training; it's about transformation.

We've helped salespeople close millions of dollars in new business simply by teaching them how to put their own solution on pause and truly listen to their customers.

We've helped leaders use the Triangle of Truth to resolve long-standing turf wars and ignite new levels of cooperation and creativity in their organizations.

The Triangle of Truth has enabled project managers to harness the collective energy and ideas of teams that were once dysfunctional and disengaged.

We've watched organizations become more productive and engaged by changing their paradigms around conflict and problem-solving.

We've had the thrill—and yes, it is a thrill for us—of watching people experience the "aha" moment as they discover that questioning, listening, and validating the other person's perspective doesn't make you less powerful; it makes you more powerful.

We've used the Triangle of Truth to help churches and families create peace where chaos once reigned. And we've created programs to help teachers use the model in their classrooms where we've seen kids as young as four learn how to solve their problems and influence their peers in a positive way.

We've seen firsthand how powerful the training and model can be.

Here's what we've discovered: You know those people out there, the ones who seem so narrow-minded, myopic, ill-informed, and stubborn? We have yet to meet a single one of them who didn't think this was a good idea. They may not be very skilled at showing it, and their approach may annoy you to death, but believe it or not, they want to solve the problem, close the deal, get the job done, and create a happy family just as much as you do.

We have a choice when it comes to other people: We can call upon their better angels, or we can continue to bring out the devil in them.

The Triangle of Truth model is simple, but it's not easy. However, if you're willing to give it a try, I think you'll discover that it's more than worth the effort.

Peace,
Lisa

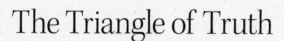

The Triangle of Truth

Tools

Download free tools at www.TriangleofTruth.com including:

- ▶ 5 Secrets of Sales Superstars: The five mind-sets that differentiate the merely competent from the simply stellar (and how you can turn your average performers into superstars by tomorrow morning)
- ▶ 10 Great Questions to Ask Your Spouse, Coworker, or Prospect
- ▶ 7 Simple Ways to Harness the Power of *And*
- ▶ How to Deal with Crazy People (Without Becoming One of Them)
- ▶ The Duality of Parenting: The Permissive vs. Controlling Quagmire
- ▶ Triangle of Truth Training Videos
- ▶ Triangle of Truth Meeting Prep Tool

For information about our workshops and seminars or to request Lisa as a keynote speaker, contact info@triangleoftruth.com.

ACKNOWLEDGMENTS

It is always a challenge to know who to thank at the end of a book. Do you thank all the writers and speakers whose work influenced your thinking? That's kind of hard because, over the course of your life, you probably assimilated a lot of ideas without even realizing it. Do you thank the individual friends, colleagues, readers, and seminar attendees who provided you with insight and perspective along the way? That can be even more challenging because you can't possibly recall every conversation, and in many instances neither you, nor they, realized that a discussion about their in-laws or boss would wind up providing fodder for a book. So perhaps it's best just to thank the Universe and be done with it.

Because, at the end of the day, you're just a writer, and it's just a book. It's not the Declaration of Independence or a blockbuster movie, and this isn't the Oscars or the Emmys. It's just a couple of pages at the back of the book that most people don't even read, and not many people outside of your family, and possibly your publisher, even care who you acknowledge or thank.

But for me, this was more than just a book. It was a chance to try to help the world become a little bit better place to be. Time will tell whether I had any impact or not. But the act of writing it has certainly changed me for the better, and for that I am extremely grateful.

It took four years to bring this book to fruition. I wasn't actively working on it the whole time, but it was always percolating in the back of my mind. I found myself gathering information in every situation I encountered and trying to get inside people's heads even more than I usually do. So it is with sincere gratitude that I thank all the people who opened their hearts and lives to me. Thank you for sharing your stories, and thank you for trusting me with your problems. I've tried to honor your intentions without violating your privacy. I hope I have succeeded.

In addition to the many people who sometimes knowingly (and sometimes unknowingly) helped me shape my ideas, there are also several individuals who have offered specific guidance and support for this project. They are:

My editor, Marian Lizzi, who believed in this idea from the moment she heard it, and whose early enthusiasm prompted me to take on the most challenging writing project of my career. I can't thank you enough for your guidance and wisdom, and for keeping me from making a mess of things. It might not seem appropriate to say you did a kick-ass job on a book devoted to peace, but you did.

My publisher, John Duff, I appreciate your continued support of my work and this project in particular.

Craig Burke, who seven years ago pulled my Forget Perfect pitches out of the DOA pile and whose single email—"These are really good!"— filled me with confidence. You might not have realized it at the time, but you prompted me to learn the ropes of PR.

My agent, Laurie Abkemeier, thank you for your frank and honest feedback, and for patiently pointing out course corrections without ever dashing the enthusiasm behind the missteps.

The experts whose examples and commentary made the book come alive: Bill Albert, Martha Beck, Chip Bell, Joe Calloway, Tahna Fischer, Julie Gilbert, Deborah Heiligman, Amy McCready, Kiki McLean, and Richard Strozzi-Heckler. Thank you for helping me connect the dots.

The peacemakers: Nancy Amestoy, Lynn McMullen, Heart Phoenix, Dot Maver, Cheryl Tarr, Terri Mansfield, and Marianne Williamson of the Peace Alliance. Thank you for igniting a spark in me that has ultimately led me to understand my true purpose on this planet.

My dear friend Lisa Daily, who thought of the title. Thank you for your endless patience with this project. You are the most fabulous friend a yakker like me could ever have. Let the record show that Lisa Daily, the Queen of Headlines, coined the phrase the *Triangle of Truth*.

Mike Alvear, a wickedly funny friend who tries to cover up his kindness with biting wit. You are fooling no one. Thank you for insisting that I do better, even when I thought I had already done enough.

The late Steve Peters, who took the time to explain the chaos theory even as he was enduring chemo.

Wynn McName, who resurfaced at the oddest of times. If you had told me twenty years ago that the W-L football star would provide thoughtful commentary on the class clown's book, I would never have believed it.

My business manager, Ellen Townsend, who kept the emails and phone calls at bay long enough for me to write, and whose continued faith in me has been a true gift.

My father, Jay Earle, who has always supported my work, and whose enthusiasm for this book was particularly appreciated. And my stepmother, Judy Earle, who, when she called me the peacemaker, validated my mission.

My husband (and business partner), Bob, who patiently served as a muse during a difficult period in his own life, and who purchased more Quik Trip coffee than one woman should be allowed to drink. It takes a strong man to put himself into service for the Universe, and it takes an even stronger one to partner up with his wife on the project. You are the kindest person I have ever known, and your constant support has meant the world to me.

My daughters, Elizabeth and Alex. You two were the game changers. After you were born, good enough was no longer good enough, and it was time for Mom to get serious about creating the kind of world she wanted you to live in. I'm not sure if I chose you, or if you chose me, but your presence has been the biggest gift of my life. You are my darling baby girls and you are powerful wise women who will one day change the world in all kinds of amazing ways that your mother can't even begin to imagine. I hope this book makes your jobs just a little bit easier.

And lastly I would like to thank you, the reader. This book was dedicated to you because I was thinking about you when I wrote it. I tried to do my best to present the material in a way that would be helpful to you, to honor your intelligence, and to speak to your best intentions. What I have asked of you is not easy, but I have every confidence that you can and will do it.

People often think I'm joking when I say that my goal is world peace. But I'm not. It *is* possible, and I see clear evidence that the arc of humanity is bending ever more quickly in that direction. At times it may seem as though the collective world has gone mad, but after talking with thousands of people, I can tell you, we are a far more compassionate lot than we give ourselves credit for.

I continue to be humbled and amazed by the loving, giving nature of people, and by the very real desire that we all have to connect.

I hope that you will join me on this journey to peace, and I hope that in some small way, I have better prepared you to do your part. You are nothing short of magnificent, and I have absolute faith that you are ready to become who you were meant to be.

THE PEACE ALLIANCE

The Peace Alliance is a national organization dedicated to empowering civic engagement toward a culture of peace. Its network includes volunteer grassroots teams in hundreds of cities, towns, and college and high school campuses across the United States.

A portion of the author's royalties from *The Triangle of Truth* is being donated to the Peace Alliance.

Visit www.ThePeaceAlliance.org for more information.

ABOUT THE AUTHOR

Lisa Earle McLeod is the founder and president of McLeod & More Inc., an international training and consulting firm, whose clients include Apple Computer, Kimberly-Clark, Pfizer, Best Buy, Deloitte, and the United Way.

An inspirational thought-leader who specializes in sales, leadership, and employee engagement, McLeod is a sought-after keynote speaker. With a broad base of experience as a sales and leadership coach, she offers surprising alternatives and incredibly practical advice that leaders and managers at every level can implement immediately. A multinational client says, "Lisa McLeod does for relationships what Steven Covey did for work habits."

McLeod writes a leadership series for Forbes.com and has been featured in the *Wall Street Journal*, *New York Times*, and *O, the Oprah Magazine*. She is a repeat guest on *Good Morning America* and makes regular radio and TV appearances.

She is the author of several books including *Forget Perfect*, the humorous personal development manifesto that continues to sell a decade after its first printing.

Lisa lives outside of Atlanta with her husband and two daughters.

For more info about Triangle of Truth training programs or to book Lisa as keynote speaker, visit www.LisaEarleMcLeod.com.